MEXICO'S
"GRAND CANYON"

The Region and the Story of the Tarahumara Indians
and the
F. C. Chihuahua al Pacífico

A RICHLY ILLUSTRATED BOOK,
PARTICULARLY OF THE
MOUNTAIN-BARRANCA SECTION
OF THIS SCENIC WONDER,
MEXICO'S "GRAND CANYON,"
THE BARRANCA DEL COBRE

---

by
JOSEPH WAMPLER

Photographs by the author except as noted.

BERKELEY, CALIFORNIA

FRONT COVER: Barranca del Cobre.
OPPOSITE: Barranca del Cobre from Divisadero.

JOSEPH WAMPLER

Box 45

Berkeley, California 94701

Printed and bound in the United States of America

Library of Congress Catalog No. 78-65783

Preface

This is a story of the complex origin of a fascinating railroad.

Take the

* °Texas, Topolobampo and Pacific Railroad and
  Telegraph Company;
* °Kansas City, Presidio del Norte and Topolobampo
  Railroad;
* °Mexican Western Railroad Company;
* Chihuahua and Pacific Railway;
* °Call and Pacific Railroad;
* Rio Grande, Sierra Madre y Pacífico;
* Kansas City, Mexico and Orient Railroad;
* Mexico Northwestern Railroad;
* Kansas City, Mexico and Orient Railroad Company;
* Kansas City, Mexico and Orient Railway Company;
* Ferrocarril Kansas City y Orient, S.A.;

combine them from here and there as potions from the minds of dreamers, hunch players, or practical and hard working engineers, or as portions of track laid and bridges built; add liberal amounts of money from time to time; mix in enough war and revolution to stun; squeeze in an all but overpowering amount of depression; add enemies and opposition at the most inconvenient times; include such a combination of peaks, ridges and gorges as to challenge the sinews of a great country; at intervals let stand and swirl and shake for ninety years.

The result is what the Tarahumaras would call a "beautiful intoxication." It is the *Ferrocarril Chihuahua al Pacífico*. What a road!

At Topolobampo you are at the sea. At Ojinaga and El Paso the plains stretch away and you are relaxed and laze along. The plateau begins at La Junta, and the foothills beyond Gonzalez. You are stimulated at Madera and Sanchez, the crests. You have come up to 8045 feet. So stop at Divisadero, here is excitement enough to tarry awhile. Refresh and prepare yourself, for the way down will be equal in feet but surpassing in experience. Here is over a hundred miles of thrills to flutter the heart and put the head in a whirl. It is more relaxing over the next hundred miles to Topolobampo, where the sight or feel of the blue waters of

---

°Never operated

the bay will put anyone into the mood of looking back and pleasant recollection. Read along and see if story, fact or picture will capture some of this for you. Better still, ride along and make it your own.

Of course there is not just a railroad spectacularly engineered through a tremendously varied terrain, which tourists visit and view with awe. There are plants and animals which in their associations and habits reflect the variety of environment. People live on the land, even throughout the country on plain, plateau, or mountain, in canyon, and some almost literally cling to the wall.

They, too, are different and interesting. They fish the sea, plow the delta soil, cut the mountain timber, graze the grassy plains, and dig for precious ore. Now, because of the railroad, this produce is exchanged more readily among themselves and shared abroad; and the people visit more frequently with each other.

Over a period of years the writer visited considerable parts of this barranca-mountain region by truck and road, mule and trail, and even afoot with the Tarahumara. As a hiker puffing up the canyon walls, a deeper appreciation of these people was gathered and felt. The trains have come and speed through along their narrow track. But as long as barrancas exist, nothing will match the easy facility of travel shown by the Tarahumara afoot in his mountain-canyon home.

My traveling companions and I have gazed with him into the evening campfire, bundled against such a chill as to have a bite and marveled at his scanty clothes. He smiled in the morning, but we have since learned that he wasn't warm at night but merely endured the cold.

To these travels I have brought training in anthropology and wildlife conservation (a branch of biology) and some years of specialization in archaeology. These disciplines (a word now very popular in academic circles and to be suspected of slight overtones of snobbery) are mentioned not to claim authority but to suggest moderate ability to distinguish the romancers from the students. For most of the text was researched, not experienced.

Further background and many pictures were gathered by a series of eight railroad trips during the past few years. My first trip would have been the first organized tour over the new railroad except for a fluke. It took a personal visit to convince the railroad official that I would hire a special train with locomotive and crew just to "Pullman camp" for several days in the barranca country among the scenery and Indians. Letters didn't do the job, so someone (not mentioned here) beat me to it. However, mine was the last private party to travel down the graded bed by truck before the rails were laid.

As a professional railroad traveler I wish to pay warm tribute to the people of Mexico, the government and railroad officials for the generous facilities they have placed at my disposal for this book. They have every right to be proud of this building achievement. In several ways they grew with the railroad.

Money was not the only problem preventing the building of the road through the Sierra Madre Occidental. However, a hundred million dollars were not easy to raise between 1871 and 1940. A number of American and British promoters learned this. And Mexico, too, found it necessary to accumulate its economic resources.

There were technical difficulties, as might be expected, and these were considered by some early builders as making the completion impossible as well as uneconomical. But as time passed techniques, equipment, engineering skills improved and were gathered by the Government of Mexico from many parts of the world. A final surge of effort during the last few construction years brought victory in 1961. Now, every blast of a diesel horn is like a hoot of triumph rolling along the barranca walls.

Among those who grew were the Tarahumara Indians. A few thousand of them were simple laborers in 1941 and used mostly hand tools. By 1960 many were skilled operators of large earth moving equipment.

Ing. Francisco M. Togno came to this railroad as a young man with a new degree. Along with the road rehabilitation and construction he built the foundation and structure of his professional career. While showing me movies of work along the *Chihuahua al Pacífico,* several times after identifiying a place, he added that a certain child of his family was born there. He spoke in warm appreciation, too, of the Tarahumara and other workers and of his technical colleagues on the enterprise. Blasting and bridging a way through this region brought men close together.

Also it made them love their country more. He made it a natural gesture to pull photographs from his personal album for me to have copied for the publisher's consideration. Very simply he said, "If it will benefit my country, it is yours." And he has secured additional photographs for use as well as other technical data studied or reproduced. The ready access to these and permission to use speeded greatly the scope and production of the book.

Another gentleman is already a second generation railroad man in this area. The father of Sr. F. J. Saenz C. worked for the *Mexican Northwestern.* One station northwest of La Junta is called Saenz. The son is now the general freight and passenger agent of the *Chihuahua al Pacífico.* This is a demanding job and usually keeps him in the office until ten at night. Still he has found the time to satisfy inconvenient requests for detailed information.

Even more important has been his concern for the comfortable and efficient operations of the rail tours. These started from a high plateau of efficiency. Hard work still goes into improving the performance over succeeding years.

In fact, I wish to include in this observation the other Mexican railroads concerned with the trips. All have done extremely well and are constantly improving. The traveler can use Mexican railroads with comfort, convenience and pleasure.

It is not wise to compare friends, particularly in their hearing. And I do have friends among the railroads used, both as to systems and personnel. So I will say simply that none of them have exceeded the performance of the *Chihuahua al Pacífico*.

The two men are mentioned because they are known to me and I have worked with them. In their several capacities they have done many things for me, but have not shown me any favoritism. True, they have gone beyond their official functions and performed friendly offices. But this is the Mexican way. So I do single them out as representing this characteristic of the Mexican people. It is not just common to railroad men, however. "Old Mexico hands" have found it throughout the country.

Now we come to a fairly typical part of many prefaces. Is there a phrase more common to them than "the brunt and heat of the day"? Those who have typed, polished, translated, proof-read, advised, cautioned, explained, and provided an effective boot of encouragement — hail to them! Theirs were not the most exciting chores, and brief preface notice represents slender reward. So, more hails plus genuine gratitude! Moreover, a number who traveled along in the high back country and helped gather some of this material bore more than the brunt and heat of the day. They even endured the chill of the night, and it was a comfort to share this. Hail again!

The treatment to follow is in weighed and measured phrases, so in the preface it is a pleasure to let the enthusiasm show.

What a railroad, what a country, what a people! Here is a kind of *Abrazo y Salud* to all.

J. W.

Table of Contents

Views inside the barranca, including the inner gorge.

The Region

What is the region through which the *F. C. Chihuahua al Pacífico* runs, and what are its major characteristics? We are concerned here with the major elements of the system, and not with spurs or projections from it. These latter, of course, are evidences of the influence of the road, of how it reaches out to draw to itself a flow of traffic from the area through which it passes. Traffic flows to it by truck, wagon, horse and mule, and even by river. In effect, the railroad constitutes a kind of traffic drainage system for the region.

The eastern terminus of the road is at Ojinaga, opposite Presidio, Texas, and near the junction of the Conchos and Rio Grande Rivers. The altitude is just under 2700 feet.

Juarez, opposite El Paso, is about 160 miles north and 125 miles west of Ojinaga, and is a thousand feet higher. Since the *Chihuahua al Pacífico* has no extension in the United States, its northern terminus is Juarez, and it is joined here by the *Ferrocarriles Nacionales de México* which reaches it by another route. Both terminals are in the the state of Chihuahua.

The western end of the road is in the state of Sinaloa at Topolobampo on the Gulf of California, 565 railroad miles from Ojinaga. The Sierra Madre Occidental intervenes. Its average crest elevation is about 6500 feet with peaks over 10,000 feet. The approach from the east is gradual except for sharper rises near the crest. The west slope is quite another thing. The drop is rapid, even precipitous at places, and the west edge of the range presents a formidable escarpment for hundreds of miles. Consequently it constitutes the greatest barrier to railroad development in this part of the world. Were it easier, the railroad would have been completed many years ago.

The eastern half of this region is essentially grassy plain area and desert country, with some inland basins. It has isolated mountains and associated with them there is some mining activity. Chihuahua is within this classification and it has had a rich mining history, with considerable activity still in progress. But essentially this is ranching and agricultural country, farming being most successful in the valleys containing streams. Railroad traffic is drawn mainly from ranch and farm activity, but with the completion of the Mountain Division there has been a considerable increase in passenger travel from Ojinaga, drawn mostly from Texas.

1

The foothills constitute a rather narrow belt at the western edge of the plains, and in some parts have important mining activity. Essentially, however, it is ranching country involved in production of grain and hay. Fruit growing is found in a number of places as well.

The Madera Section of the rail system has plains, foothills, plateaus, mountains, and inland basins and deserts in the north. The southern section follows for a considerable distance the Papigochic River, a branch of the Yaqui. This has been prosperous agricultural country for years and now has a series of small towns based on this industry, which is the main source of traffic.

Here the Papigochic River has encroached into the eastern drainage system and thus has moved many miles east through the crest of the mountain range. Consequently to move north out of this drainage, it is necessary to cross the mountain to reach the basin country. Here the range is high, and Madera is actually the highest point on the entire railroad.

The early railroads went into this area initially to get the traffic of mines and timber. The largest lumber mills in Mexico were conveniently situated on lower slopes. These mills in the mountains have worked much of the original growth, and the lumber and mining industries still provide the major rail business.

Northeast of the mountains is basin country. Nuevo Casas Grandes is the economic center of this area which is principally agricultural. It, too, has been a prosperous farming region for centuries and its fertile soil attracted many Mormon colonists in the latter part of the nineteenth century. Passenger traffic here has been moderate, but will increase with the improvement of the line which is now in progress.

Southwest, out of La Junta, the road quickly passes through the foothills, mainly ranching country, and gets into the mountain barranca region after passing over the plateau or uplands. There are several sawmill towns along the way. The milling activity from the adjacent areas has been reduced by reason of a scarcity of standing timber and controlled cutting, supervised by the government agency concerned. However, logs continue to arrive from more remote areas, so lumber is an important item of freight.

The mining potential which the railroad opens is impossible to estimate, but it could be immense. For example, an operation recently closed at La Bufa, principally a copper mine, employed in its optimum period a thousand miners and reduction plant operators, and justified the building and maintaining of 85 miles of road across the plateau and into Batopilas Canyon.

Then there are the great silver mines at Batopilas, 15 miles down-stream. These were not *worked* out, but *put* out of operation by the effects of the revolution of 1910. At the turn of the century one mine alone required five hundred mules to operate a system of relays to transport ore and supplies between the mine and Chihuahua.

As for the region to the west, so much ore potential exists that if you stop at a place for a short time, someone is almost bound to approach you with samples and an assay sheet and attempt to raise money or sell stock. The railroad is certain to have much mine operation traffic from this area.

The barranca scenery is so grand that an increasing number of tourists ride the railroad to see it. Passenger traffic has increased to such an extent in five years that service and facilities have had to be expanded to accommodate it. And it is bound to grow as interest in the area increases.

The Maritime plain, west from the foothills, is thorn brush country above the irrigation project and rich, fat land below. Climate and water, supplied by irrigation, make several crops a year possible. So the needs of the agriculture industry develop a need for increasing freight service in this section.

What about the port at Topolobampo? It too represents a comparatively untapped potential, but more harbor facilities are in development to attract more seagoing exchange of goods. Even at this little developed stage one can observe that a substantial increase has taken place in business during the past five years.

The *F. C. Chihuahua al Pacífico* has already resulted in a great movement of travel and produce up and down its system, and to the sea and beyond.

In addition, there is the exchange of traffic with other railroads. There is a junction with the *F. C. Pacífico* in the west at San Blas; and at Chihuahua with the *National Railways of Mexico*. At Ojinaga-Presidio in the east, it ties in with the *Santa Fe Railway*, a parent road for a short time. In the north, at Juarez-El Paso, it meets again with the *National Railways of Mexico*. And a crossing of the border make possible a junction with the following rail systems of the United States: *Santa Fe Railway*, *Southern Pacific*, and *Texas and Pacific*.

So between the *F. C. Chihuahua al Pacífico* and its environs there exists a fine symbiotic relationship. The railroad helps to open and develop the region, and the region gives strength to the road.

Railroad Story

THE DREAM

Albert Kimsey Owen was born about 1848 in Chester, Pennsylvania. His father, Dr. Joshua K. Owen, was Senior Surgeon of Volunteers in the Civil War, serving under General Ben Butler; and was a personal friend of President Abraham Lincoln, General Ulysses S. Grant, and many other influential men of his day. His mother died during his childhood, and because of his remarkable father, he and his older brother Alfred received exceptional latitude to take advantage of the opportunities of the times.

So it was that while in their early teens, the two brothers served as orderlies on the General Staff of the Army of the Potomac. For two years they followed this army, enduring the privations and exposures of soldiers, and witnessing the battles and horrors of war.

Further rough education was provided by a trip into the West with their father, again with the army. They met Kit Carson at Los Pinos, Colonel Bowie at El Paso, passed through the country of the Navajo, and visited and traded in the lodges of the chiefs of the Cheyennes, Comanches, Kiowas, and Arapahoes. A short time later these, and other plains tribes, were at war with the whites under the command of General Blunt.

More adventure and training followed, for Dr. Owen was diligent about the education of his sons. In April 1866, shortly after the end of the Civil War, they left for fourteen months of travel in Europe, Palestine, and Egypt. Three thousand miles of this pilgrimage was made on foot, and this gave them the opportunity to increase their powers of observation. Albert extended this journey, walking 800 miles through England, Scotland, and Ireland, and returned to Pennsylvania at the age of 19.

Shortly thereafter he began his on-the-job-training for a career in civil engineering. An increasing amount of this work took the form of railroad surveying, and eventually he arrived in Colorado. There his talents impressed General William J. Palmer, closely associated with the Denver and Rio Grande Railroad, and he was invited by Palmer to go to Mexico. General Palmer and General William S. Rosecrans had engaged him to investigate the possibility of a railroad to central Mexico along the west coast through Sonora to Colorado Springs. During eleven months, Owen traveled 5000 miles, about 3400 on horseback. The remaining distance was covered aboard small coastal sloops and steamers, for the purpose of investigating harbor facilities.

4

One of his traveling companions was General Manuel Gonzales, who ten years later, was to become President of Mexico. On this trip he also met Dr. Benjamin R. Carmen, the United States Consul to Mazatlán, through whom he first learned of Topolobampo.

Whatever the nature of his report to Generals Palmer and Rosecrans, Owen did not return to Topolobampo until September of the following year. At this time, an examination of the bay and its surroundings impressed him that Topolobampo was soon to become a port facility for the exchange of trade between the peoples of the world. Just recall that at this time there was no Panama Canal, and only one transcontinental railroad, recently completed. Owen's dream was to shorten, by over 400 miles, the freighting distance between the midwest and the deep water harbors of the Pacific Coast.

He and engineer Fred Fitch, followed up these observations by riding 100 miles inland to El Fuerte, thereby familiarizing themselves with the route, and the developmental potential of the region. These impressions increased Owen's enthusiasm and eloquence. Therefore, this magnetic young man of twenty-four apparently had little difficulty in persuading Don Blas Ibarra and Dr. Benjamin Carmen to file a claim to 111,000 acres of land, including the harbor area. Fitch was to have 5% for the necessary surveying; Carlos Retas, son-in-law of Ibarra, 5% for legal work; Owen 20%; and the remainder to Ibarra and Carmen. Owen, however, was given complete power of attorney from all parties; from this key position he now set about promoting the project.

One of the first steps was to present, in May 1873, before the Governor's Convention of the Southern States in Atlanta, Georgia, an extensive plan for a railroad to be built from Norfolk, Virginia, via Austin, Texas, to Topolobampo. The plan was approved, but the hard times of the seventies prevented its execution.

Another step was to press the project before the old family friend, President Ulysses S. Grant. As a consequence, Commodore (later Admiral) George W. Dewey, was assigned to survey and map Topolobampo Bay.

By 1873 the consent of the Mexican Government had been arranged. Now began some of the major promotional efforts. An adequately sponsored proposal was presented to both Houses of Congress in December 1874, as a "Memorial of A. K. Owen, Civil Engineer — The Great Southern Trans-Oceanic and International Air Line — Asia to Europe via Mexico and the United States." It urged this shorter route be developed with "Treasury Money"— Greenback currency.

About this time Owen became involved in a number of various social reform projects, an activity which undoubtedly had important bearing upon his promotional ventures. He was on the organizing board of the first "Greenback Club" of Pennsylvania, wrote articles on monetary reform, free trade, and equal suffrage for women.

His railroad project, however, was in conflict with the powerful transcontinental railroad groups of that day. Influential friends notwithstanding, Owen was unable to compete with the powerful forces of these groups.

Between 1873 and 1879, much of his energy was given to urging his projects before Congress. At the same time he was obliged to earn his living from civil engineering.

Whether from excess of discouragement or abundance of energy, Owen in 1879, just past thirty, again went to Mexico. This time he was highly represented to President Porfirio Díaz. And again, by force of personality and the scope and practicality of his ideas, he won the concession to drain the Valley of Mexico and build the railroad from Mexico City to El Paso. In a short time he lost this concession.

The railroad, however, was no longer the primary effort. Rather, it was now just a part of a socialistic endeavor which he called "Integral Co-operation." This envisioned a Utopian Colony to be established in Northern Sinaloa where Owen and colleagues had already established vast concessions. The idea was immensely popular and won a great deal of notice through newspaper and magazine accounts, and lecture programs both in the United States and abroad. The railroad plan shared indirectly in this burst of interest. At least the idea had been planted, and cultivation continued. General Manuel Gonzales, who was one of Owen's traveling companions in 1871 along the Northwest Coast of Mexico, was now President of Mexico. Through his good offices, he secured a concession in 1881 to construct a railroad from Topolobampo across the Sierra, called the "Texas, Topolobampo and Pacific Railroad and Telegraph Company": mileage involved, two thousand; subsidy, sixteen million dollars; chief engineer, Owen.

Again Owen interested General Ulysses S. Grant and his son, along with many other prominent people. Practical results were limited however, because most of Owen's energies were consumed by his colonizing efforts. Of the projected route, one hundred miles were located from the sea inland by 1883. By February 1885, clearing of the right-of-way and grading inland from the hills at Topolobampo had begun. A small party was working on survey and cutting line for the right-of-way near Topolobampo in November of 1886.

Shortly afterwards, Owen developed some doubts about the existing organization's means for building the railroad. He met with the Kansas City Council in 1888, and presented a proposal for a "Kansas City, Presidio del Norte and Topolobampo Railroad." One purpose for this was to center interest in the colony in the Mid-west.

The problems of the colony subordinated the railroad development. Nevertheless, the Mexican Government renewed Owen's concession on June 7, 1890. In August, an English syndicate contracted to build the road from Topolobampo to Texas. Hope and optimism again were high.

This arrangement was short-lived. By July 1891, the British syndicate was "out" and the "Mexican Western Railroad Company" was "in." This was an association of American businessmen incorporated in Colorado. Owen was given the contract for surveying and construction.

Owen and a few companions rode over the proposed route in September 1891. This was the difficult 155-mile stretch of mountain-barranca terrain between Agua Caliente de Lanphar and Sisoquichic. His description of the trip includes some incredibly naive observations for an engineer! "I was impressed by the few difficulties to be met in the construction of a railroad through the Canyon of the Sententrion from Guoza to Bocoyna — tunnels will not be necessary; light grades, little cost compared with east and west trunk lines already across the same chain, the Rocky and Cascade Mountains of the United States." Certainly this is a dreamer speaking, not an engineer, for this is roughly the route of the existing line, which took another seventy years and much modern engineering ingenuity to complete. The principal bridges and tunnels in the mountain region total more than seventy, one tunnel being over one mile in length. Soon after this trip, colony problems multiplied. As a consequence of a fateful meeting between Owen and other colony leaders in May 1893, Owen left and never returned. He continued to promote the idea by lecturing and writing, but after 1903, did not figure in colony affairs. But he did remain active in railroad affairs.

His concession was renewed in 1897, and in 1899 he arranged with Enrique C. Creel of the *Chihuahua al Pacífico* to extend that line to Topolobampo. Contrary to a contention of Arthur E. Stilwell, who figures next in the story, one author claims that he interested Stilwell and Kansas City bankers in organizing the *Kansas City, Mexico and Orient Railway* in 1900, and made use of his good offices with high Mexican officials for this purpose. Further, he took great interest in the construction which began in 1903.

THE BUILDING

KANSAS CITY, MEXICO AND ORIENT RAILROAD

It is small wonder that ninety years passed between the dream on the beach of Topolobampo and the unbroken thread of rails between Kansas City and the Gulf of California. The promotional problems were tremendous, and required the support, over the vicissitudes of some decades, of a small army of the most influential men in both countries. There were powerful forces of opposition. Financing was followed by refinancing, organization by reorganization. Wars intervened, and revolutions were destructive and disruptive. Building this railroad had become a "spectacular," and the final act was an extending challenge even for such a great country as Mexico. This act climaxed in the building of the road through the mountain-barranca country of the Sierra Madre Occidental.

A drop of 7000 feet must be made in 122 miles. The engineers tunneled through mountains and flung bridge spans across great streams, gouged out the sides of vast ridges to produce great fills, and wound the roadbed through, under, and over, in countless curves and loops until down, down, down, and the job was done. The President of Mexico came to the dedication with distinguished guests, and all said it was a good job, a spectacular thing, and a beauty worthy of all the toil. Speeches were made, bands played, prayers were prayed, and the dream had become a structural reality. The road was officially opened on November 23, 1961.

Arthur Stilwell has been called the builder of the Orient Railroad. This, and the even shorter name *Orient*, is frequently used to refer to the *Kansas City, Mexico and Orient Railroad*, or the several variations of the name, as a consequence of subsequent reorganizations. In fact, locomotives of the system often had in big letters on the tender, just the word *Orient*. Stilwell implies that he regarded this railroad his own idea, dream, or "hunch." Whatever the basis of this claim, it would seem remarkable that an alert railroad man would have no knowledge of the activities of Albert Kimsey Owen, since some of Owen's activities, in the late '90's, centered in Kansas City, Stilwell's home. But there is no point in attempting to resolve these conflicting claims. The story is complex enough as it is.

Arthur Stilwell had lost control of "his" railroad, the *Kansas City, Pittsburgh and Gulf,* shortly prior to a testimonial dinner given him at the Midland Hotel, Kansas City, on February 11, 1900. The dinner was an expression of esteem on the part of friends, admirers and stockholders, of Stilwell's ventures, and was also thought of as a means for his graceful departure from the railroad scene. Contrary to expectations, Stilwell electrified his audience by making a speech which proposed the formation of a new railroad from Kansas City to a deep water port on the West Coast, which would reduce, by about 400 miles, the distance between the Midwest and the Pacific Ocean. The route comprised about 1610 miles between Kansas City and "Port Stilwell" on Topolobampo Bay, Sinaloa, Mexico. Once again he demonstrated that he was a superb promoter, a consumate salesman, and a man of action.

The very next day he met with Dr. Woods and Church White of the Bank of Commerce, and financial groundwork was laid. Soon afterward, Stilwell headed for Mexico.

In Chihuahua City he met with Enrique C. Creel, who was building a railroad between Chihuahua and Miñaca. This road, the *Chihuahua and Pacific,* had operated its first train from Chihuahua to the end of the track at Santa Isabel, 33 miles west, on July 15, 1899. And the line was opened to Miñaca on May 20, 1900, a short time after Stilwell's visit. The success of this venture increased Creel's enthusiasm for Stilwell's larger plan. He joined it with enthusiasm, added his facilities to the project, and accepted a vice-presidency in the new railroad. Moreover, he used his influence to aid Stilwell in Mexico City, where meetings with President Porfirio Díaz culminated in the granting of a concession. *The Kansas City, Mexico and Orient Railroad* was incorporated in Kansas City on May 1, 1900, and legalized in Mexico soon thereafter.

Since the financial houses of the East were now in poor repute with Stilwell, his aim was to do the bulk of the financing in the Midwest and as much as possible among small investors. Towns and communties along the route contributed or invested substantial sums. Enthusiasm was particularly high in Kansas, Oklahoma, and Texas. Some parts of these states had no rail communication and were anxious to get it. And there were some English investors too, who saw the potential in the plan.

Actual construction was scheduled in five sections, two in the United States, and three in Mexico. Those in Mexico were: (1) East from Chihuahua City; (2) West from the Chihuahua and Pacific track end at Miñaca; (3) Northeast from Topolobampo.

In early 1902 grading began. The first rail was laid in Mexico in late March of 1902. By April 30, 1903, trains ran between Chihuahua and

Trancas, 35 miles northeast. During this month three locomotives were sent to Mexico. This activity, plus the work in the United States, made a vigorous beginning.

In 1903 most of the line was located. The grades east of Chihuahua were 1½%; east of Topolobampo up the Fuerte Valley a 1% grade was required. The first plan called for 40 miles of cog railway over a 14% maximum grade going into the Sierra Madre Mountains. Later surveying, however, located a 5% grade line, and subsequent work located three closely adjacent routes with 2½% gradient. The final plan, then, included grades up to 2½%. This required considerable use of curves, and contemplated several loops; also 10 or 15 tunnels. At one place the line circles back under itself and makes a complete loop. This was completed near Pitorreal, about 40 miles west of Creel. It was utilized by the engineers when the tracks were laid in the early 40's and is one of three such examples found along North American railroads.

The total length of the Sierra grade from Sanchez (7 miles west of Creel) to San Pedro (about 122 miles west of Sanchez on the existing railroad) was estimated to be about 200 miles. However, this proposed route was not the route used when the railway was completed in 1961. This is demonstrated by the fact that the Sierra grade required not ten or fifteen tunnels as originally planned, but 68 tunnels, from 94 to 5,928 feet in length, and 27 bridges, 103 to 1638 feet in length. Obviously, rougher terrain was traversed to achieve the shorter route in 1961. This difficult area, then, was deferred for a sound combination of financial, promotional, and engineering reasons. The work proceeded more rapidly elsewhere.

On the western end of the line, the management opened 62 miles of road between Topolobampo and Fuerte. Then, in early 1905 work was completed between Miñaca and Sanchez, 7 miles southwest of Creel. Since Sanchez lies at 8045 feet, where the western descent begins, was proof enough that some formidable mountain country was conquerable. And this was encouraging, for the most difficult terrain of mountain and barranca was ahead – the Sierra section, Sanchez to the Fuerte River.

The eastern section in Mexico showed more modest progress. The road was completed in 1908 between Trancas and Falomir, 84 miles northeast of Chihuahua. This represented a net gain of only 49 miles since early 1903, through relatively easy country. And by March 1911 services varied from daily to tri-weekly.

From this time on it is not difficult to observe a considerable loss of steam in the operation and construction of the system. The major problem, of course, was financial. In addition, revolution in Mexico and World War I soon added to the difficulties.

One of Stilwell's building contractors for the Western Chihuahua Section was Pancho Villa. Stilwell admitted to feeling personally unsympathetic towards Villa. What Villa felt towards Stilwell is not recorded. Perhaps a fact of significance is that Superintendent Juan F. Treviño fled from his office to El Paso for the two years Villa controlled Chihuahua. In any event, the revolution stopped building in Mexico.

The financial difficulties produced the first of a series of crises in the United States. On March 7, 1912, the *Kansas City, Mexico and Orient Railroad* went into receivership and Arthur Stilwell was ousted.

The receivers got 950.6 miles of railway, of which the Mountain Section in Mexico was in the best condition, although 60 pound rails had been used there. In the United States, mostly 70-75-pound rails had been used, and these were spiked to untreated ties with little ballast. The 75 miles between Falomir and the Rio Grande had been graded, but the unsettled political conditions precluded further construction. Nor could work be done on the Sierra Section. In 1912, construction cost for this section was estimated as high as $500,000 per mile for the approximate 200 miles as routed. The actual building cost, from 1943 through 1960, was roughly $54,175,000 even though the shorter route was used.

Some improvement was shown in the United States' portion of the system by 1915, for on June 30, the receivers were discharged. Conditions for the Mexican portion showed no marked change.

A reorganization plan was put into effect on December 8, 1915, and the new corporation was chartered as the *Kansas City, Mexico and Orient Railroad Company,* which absorbed the *Kansas City, Mexico and Orient Railroad,* and other facilities. The Mexican situation was still too unstable to encourage construction even if the money had been available. And the financial situation deteriorated further as a result of World War I.

So on April 16, 1917, the parent company again went into receivership, but the *Orient of Texas* was returned to its owners.

Following the new receivership, the Mexico Pacific Division struggled along and operated a tri-weekly mixed service in the Fuerte Valley when no armed conflict was in progress between Fuerte and the coast. Villa's revolutionaries and other armies were constantly tearing up the track between Falomir, Chihuahua, and Sanchez, consequently service was irregular. By 1923, such a series of problems had developed that the road came close to failing completely.

It was saved only by a lucky combination of factors: Labor took a reduction of wages, connecting carriers granted a reduction in rates paid by the Orient on interline traffic, and Interstate Commerce Commission prescribed an increased share of joint revenues. A number of local governments reduced taxes. In Mexico, most of the track in Chihuahua was a financial drain, since it was out of operation, while the line in operation in Sinaloa was self-sustaining.

But the road was really saved by oil. Two tank cars of oil were loaded at Fort Stockton in 1922. The Santa Rita well "blew in" on May 28, 1923, at Big Lake. *The Orient* transported great quantities of oil until pipe lines were completed to do this job, but the greatest benefit was from general freight revenues following the increased prosperity of the region due to oil.

Then a partial reorganization once again took place, in the form of a forced sale on March 27, 1924, before the increased prosperity enabled repayment of a government loan. The same management remained, but the road again got a new name, the *Kansas City, Mexico and Orient Railway Company*. How practical it was, then, just to have *Orient* painted on the tenders of the locomotives!

Increased prosperity provided more money for everything. The advertising for 1925 was $1,711 as compared to $4 for 1923. Very substantial improvement was made on maintenance of roadbed and equipment. The income increased, and by 1927 oil accounted for 48% of the road's income. In 1924 the Mexican government had given some aid to the railroad as partial repayment of damage due to the revolution. Seven carloads of rails reached Falomir, and the Conchos bridge opened. A great amount of rehabilitation work was completed. In 1925 the Mountain Division was restored, so that trains ran two or three times a week between Creel and Miñaca, the junction point with the *Mexico Northwestern*.

The Pacific Division began construction of a new line between Fuerte and San Pedro in 1926. Rehabilitation in the Chihuahua area resulted in a twice weekly mixed train service as far as Pulpito, 92 miles east of Chihuahua, by spring of 1927. So considerable progress was made to get the railroad well along toward a unified operation. This prospect was brightened in January 1928, when Congress authorized the bridging of the Rio Grande near Presidio, Texas. But soon the Mexican part of the system was to be separated from the parent road in the United States.

On September 24, 1928, the *Santa Fe Railway* gained financial control of the Orient. The Santa Fe management decided to dispose of the Orient holdings in Mexico before beginning the integration of the United

States section of the system. So the three Mexican divisions were sold to Benjamin F. Johnston and the *United Sugar Company* of Los Mochis, Sinaloa. Johnson put up $650,000 in cash and gave a mortgage of $900,000 in bonds. He received 16 locomotives and other equipment assigned to Mexico, and 316 miles of railway, 95 miles of which were new.

A gap in the line still existed north of the border. It was closed, and the first train rolled into the border town of Presidio, Texas, in October 1930. And as a consequence of a span of 1960 feet of open-deck pile trestle across the Rio Grande, it was now possible for a box of sawmill equipment to leave Kansas City and traverse the completed route to the crest of the Sierra Madre Occidental before it was unloaded at Creel, Chihuahua. But the difficult Sierra section between Creel and San Pedro remained incomplete.

The *Santa Fe* continued to strengthen and restore track and equipment north of the border. Service was expanded. The *Orient* weathered the depression and grew stronger under the wings of the *Santa Fe*. But on June 30, 1941, the parent *Kansas City, Mexico and Orient Railway Company* ceased to exist corporately, as a consequence of a merger with the *Santa Fe Railway*.

Meanwhile, south of the border, in 1928, the so-called "Johnston Railroad" had become the *Ferrocarril Kansas City y Oriente, S.A.* Soon thereafter, Johnston and L. Roy Hoard, president of the *Mexico Northwestern Railway,* joined forces, combined the construction and administration of the Northwestern and Oriente railroads under Hoard, and moved the operating terminal to La Junta. The economies which resulted enabled both roads to survive the depression, but neither made any money.

The close of this phase was hastened by the death of Benjamin F. Johnston in March, 1937, while on a world cruise. The Johnston heirs soon began looking for a buyer for the railroad. Negotiations towards purchase were authorized in 1939 by the Secretary of the Treasury of Mexico. Transfer of the *Kansas City, Mexico y Oriente, S.A.* was made in the spring of 1940. The settlement included a modest payment for cancellation of the *Santa Fe* mortgage.

Several immediate changes resulted. The *Oriente* operations were separated from those of the *Mexican Northwestern,* and Don Juan Treviño was reinstated as manager of the former. And La Junta became the junction instead of Miñaca, after the government purchased the linking trackage from the Mexican Northwestern.

THE REALITY

By spring of 1940 when the government acquired the *Ferrocarril Kansas City y Oriente, S.A.,* much money had been spent, great energy and work applied, and many years had passed, but Owen's dream was not fulfilled. The gap remained; the mountain-barranca section was unfinished. To finish it, and to rehabilitate the existing road, constituted the major problem and the supreme challenge. Another twenty years of national exertion remained.

We have been developing an account of the construction of a railroad between Ojinaga, Chihuahua and Topolobampo, Sinaloa. In a sinuous way, the line goes from a point in the east towards another point in the west about 565 miles away. However, there is a gap in the story. Over a hundred miles has not been constructed; the Sierra section. In addition, another deviation from the dream of a single parent railroad from Kansas City to Topolobampo is the railroad from Chihuahua City west to La Junta. The *Kansas City, Mexico y Oriente* operated this road, but corporately it was still the *Mexico Northwestern.* Over a period of years the latter road developed a line which made a long looping curve from Chihuahua towards the northwest and then back northeast to reach Juarez (opposite El Paso) 235 miles almost due north of Chihuahua. It is now a part of the *F. C. Chihuahua al Pacífico* system. How did this come about?

On May 10, 1887, Luis Huller received a sort of multiple concession to build railroads in northwest Mexico. One part was concerned with rights to build a line between Juarez, Corralitos and Magdalena. The part between Juarez and Corralitos was completed September 18, 1897. Soon after, the Rio Grande, Sierra Madre y Pacífico was organized to operate the system, which had been extended through Casas Grandes to Pearson. Since the construction progress lagged, the concession to extend the line was cancelled in 1900.

In the meantime, another project was undertaken in the Chihuahua area to the south. The *Call and Pacific Railroad* had secured a concession in November 1894. A portion of these rights was purchased in March 1897 by Enrique Creel and Alfred Spendlove. This permitted them to build a single line between Chihuahua and the coast of southern Sonora. They were vigorous in developing their rights.

The survey started soon after in 1897, and construction began on March 25, 1898. The road was incorporated in New Jersey on April 13,

1898, as the *Chihuahua and Pacific Railroad Company*. On July 15, 1899 the first Chihuahua and Pacific train left Chihuahua City and ran to the end of the track at Santa Isabel, 33 miles west. The line was opened between Chihuahua and Miñaca on May 20, 1900, and in August of 1900 Creel and Spendlove relinquished the concession to continue through to the coast. Either the mountains and barrancas were too difficult, or they may have been better disposed towards Owen's route to Topolobampo. Soon afterwards, Stilwell's project for the *Orient* seemed to combine the concessions of Owen and the *Call and Pacific* concession of Creel. This development, the *Kansas City, Mexico and Orient,* was carried along in the account above, and needs no further treatment here.

But Creel expanded the *Chihuahua and Pacific* to the northwest by getting a concession in 1904, to construct a line between El Carpio (La Junta) and Temosachic. This line was opened in July 1905.

British capital came into the story. The *Mexico Northwestern Railroad* had acquired the rights of the *Rio Grande, Sierra Madre y Pacífico* and added to these on October 19, 1909, the *Chihuahua and Pacific Railroad Company*. These concessions were consolidated on November 22, 1909. Also included were additional rights to build a road from Madera to Juarez, and to complete the system between La Junta-Madera-Juarez. Subsequently this was done and the road operated as the *Mexico Northwestern* until May 27, 1952, when the government took possession and integrated the system. Nevertheless, this left a loose end to be picked up, in proper order. The operation was now in government hands, but the name had not disappeared.

Commemorative sign near Santa Barbara where completed railroad was opened. F. C. Chihuahua al Pacífico photo.

15

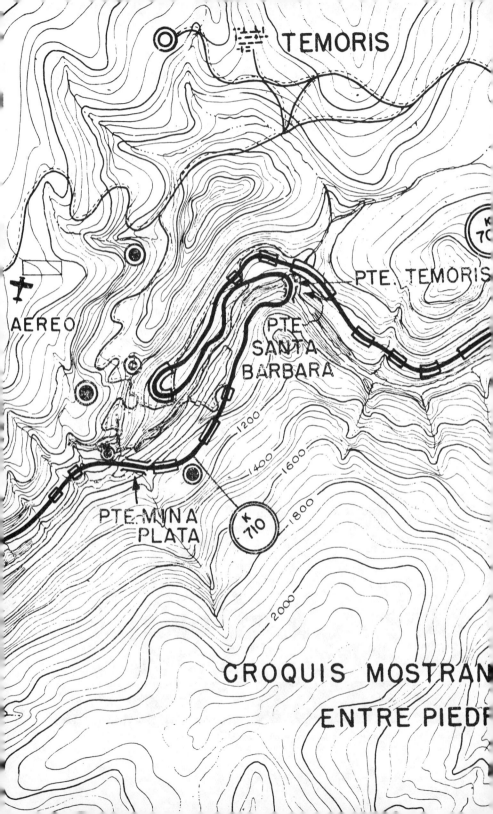

F. C. CHIHUAHUA al PACIFICO

When the Government of Mexico acquired the *F. C. Kansas City, Mexico y Oriente, S.A.* from the Johnston estate in the spring of 1940, the railroad and equipment received showed the effects of war, revolution, depression, and shifting management. Rehabilitation of the existing line was more important than building new roadbed in the forbidding mountains. Still, the idea of connecting the system by construction of the missing link, the Sierra Division, was pushed along with increasing vigor. Each new President promised work towards completion, and progress gathered momentum. The mountainous ramparts finally fell to the assaults of the Mexican people.

In the meantime, it was not enough simply to restore the existing railroad to its former status of operation. True, it would have to be put back into economical condition to serve the region. But it would also have to be prepared as a fitting accompaniment to the national achievement of traversing the hitherto unconquerable mountain-barrancas. To do this by the highest standards was highly commendable; to exceed them was to show leadership.

It was done this way. The world was searched for engineering ideas, techniques and equipment. These were tested and applied. The result was not only a scenic marvel, but a spectacular engineering feat. This was not done in a day, nor a decade.

Service over the Chihuahua Division during the 1940's was essentially tri-weekly mixed trains from Chihuahua on Mondays, Wednesdays, and Fridays, and return trips on succeeding days. When necessary, additional service was added. Traffic began to increase and more freight was exchanged across the border.

The Creel Division was more prosperous too, and offered similar service. Both mining and lumbering freight increased, and larger shipments reached war-inflated markets in the United States.

The Pacific Division was less prosperous. A surfaced road between Los Mochis and San Blas hurt the railroad, but it had considerable traffic when the crops moved from field to market. Thus, good business was enjoyed for a half of each year. In brief, the railroad on the whole, met the demands put upon it, and prepared for the future.

Rehabilitation began in the year in which the purchase was made, and 88 kilometers were completed before the close of 1940. In 1941, an additional 145 kilometers were completed, and the route in the Septen-

Tunnels and terraces near Santa Barbara on topographical map.   **17**
(Secretaria de Obras Publicas, Memoria de la Construccion del
Ferrocarril al Pacífico).

trion River area was surveyed. Improvement of the line as to bed, tunnel, and grade required that a new survey be made for 140 kilometers out of Miñaca. This and some grading between Creel and Ciuteco was done in 1943.

At this time the means of accomplishing the work were limited. Heavy equipment, at first, totaled two bulldozers. The laborers had hand tools — picks, shovels, crowbars, sledges and bits, and explosives. There were 2000 to 3000 workers, mostly Tarahumaras. Naturally the progress was slow, but increased about 1956 when more money was available for equipment.

Construction peaked in 1960. Then in use were 50 shovels, 120 compressors, 500 jack hammers, and 60 bulldozers. The laborers and operators totaled about 2000 and many of these were still Tarahumaras. A number of them, who had literally "girded up their loins" in 1941, now wore jeans and rode heavy equipment as operators in 1960.

A register of the yearly results has the sound of the battle roll of a famous regiment:

1944 established line between Sanchez and Pitorreal; rehabilitation work between Creel and Sanchez; access roads completed in region of Temoris

1945 work intensified in Mountain Division

1946

1947 more grading and rehabilitation

1948 eleven tunnels finished, totaling 908 meters

1949 grading completed between San Pedro and Topolobampo; buildings constructed at San Blas

1949

to construction work suspended, but reconstruction continued;

1953 rehabilitation work

1954 rehabilitation work done between Topolobampo-San Pedro, Ojinaga-Chihuahua, La Junta-Juarez; construction work only on grading and drainage

1955 constructed 53 kilometers of grades; relocated 170 kilometers of access roads so as not to obstruct construction route.

The year 1955 was important for legal and organizational reasons. The *Mexico Northwestern Railroad* was absorbed by the *F. C. Chihuahua al Pacífico*, which finally represented, in name, the whole. Soon it would connect with the west and unite the elements of the system into a single operational unit.

1956 construction work on drainage, bridges, access roads and facilities

1957 work intensified, six bridges built and six tunnels dug; also reconstruction work

1958 built 22 kilometers of grade and 1500 meters of grade and drains; constructed 5 tunnels and 3 bridges; worked on foundations of 3 big bridges; rehabilitated 180 kilometers of old road (much of this between Chihuahua and Miñaca, the former *Chihuahua and Pacific Railroad*) and put into operation.

The tempo of work kept increasing as more money became available. Activity in many places, and of many sorts, was carried on to bring the road together after the completion of the Mountain Section.

Before this was accomplished, in the spring of 1960, the writer with companions went through on special permit provided by the supervising engineer in charge. We had a two-ton truck and a pick-up with camper. For a number of miles out of Creel we rolled over the railroad bed shortly before the rails were laid. This was easy and a speed of 35 miles per hour was possible. We passed through cuts, over fills and small bridges, and blew the horns when traveling through tunnels.

A few miles beyond Divisadero we encountered the first work crews. Then the procedure changed. At times we traveled on the railroad bed, at other times on detours along the sides. These became more numerous and longer, until we were obliged to use the access roads for stretches of several miles. These long detours by-passed areas of heavy construction in progress, as curious tourists could not be allowed to delay the functioning of many men and costly equipment.

A number of times we reached headquarters of construction organizations; a good many private companies were used. At these places our authorization for our presence was requested, and permission of the engineer in charge was required before we could proceed. Permission to continue was always given with courtesy, but we were never invited to stop for coffee.

One place of long detour was around Temoris, which came as no surprise. On the other side of the mountain, the terrain provided the engineer with a major problem. Here at Santa Barbara, even a person ignorant of engineering can appreciate and marvel at how the railroad was brought through the mountain and along the side by successively lower loops, before the Septentrion River was crossed by a curving bridge which reversed the direction of descent.

So we did not see this, but the next morning after a camp-out, we traveled some miles to the Chinipas River where the bridge foundations neared completion. Soon we traveled the railbed again.

Between the drainages of the Chinipas and Fuerte Rivers a tunnel had been bored through the intervening mountain. To get through to the other side, we drove our trucks into the black opening of the famous El Descano tunnel. We did not know it then but suspected it, and had the lights on from the beginning — they were definitely necessary. It was not necessary to blow the horns, but it reassured us to do so at increasingly frequent intervals. When the tunnel exit first faintly appeared, we were grateful indeed; to back up more than a mile before oncoming work vehicles was an experience devoutly not to be wished.

Soon after the completion of this excursion into the bowels of the earth (it was dark in there and easy to imagine rumblings), we reached the Fuerte River, and the water was just low enough for the pick-up to cross at a prepared fording place, provided that the speed was not such as to produce a consequential wave. We deferred the examination and photographing of the Fuerte Bridge foundations until safely on the other side.

There were no more rivers to cross and after traveling a few miles through the foothills, we came to the beginning of the wide Maritime plain, where the rails from the crossing of the mountains were being joined to those coming from the coast at Topolobampo.

1959 lots of work at many places along the line, but concentrated in the Mountain Section

1960 the tempo greatly accelerated, with tremendous activity in the Mountain Section; rail laying began in the latter half of the year

1961 rail laying greatly increased because El Presidente was coming

1961 *November 23* — El Presidente came on the presidential train with many guests from Mexico and abroad, and ceremonially opened the railroad. The rails from east and west had joined.

The ceremony took place in a spectacular setting near Santa Barbara (Temoris). A memorial was made of a frame of rails from the old road, hung with stainless steel letters two feet high. These tell the story of the event for all who pass by to see. It is located near the border, or state boundary. This is fitting and symbolic, for a new artery of economic life between the states of Chihuahua and Sinaloa and, broadly speaking, all Mexico was joined here.

So speeches were made, bands played, and the diesels hooted their horns.

It is not inappropriate to refer to a railroad as an organic thing. It is inanimate to be sure, but it has qualities common to living things. Organic tissues have their function or work. They do their work, develop wear, and must be restored in order to remain healthy. So it is with a railroad.

It is built and works, and while it works, it is constantly being maintained and restored by new construction, reconstruction, and rehabilitation if it is to remain a healthy organism.

The *F. C. Chihuahua al Pacífico* is not only a healthy, but a growing railroad. While it carries its present load of freight and passengers, it is preparing to carry more. So while the wheels roll to do this work, there is construction and reconstruction to maintain operational efficiency and to increase the facilities of the road. A project now, of high priority, is the improvement of port facilities at Topolobampo. There is no doubt that the dream of Owen has been realized; and the port may exceed, in population and size, his dream of 1872 on the lonely sands of Topolobampo Bay.

OUTLINE OF FORMING AND BUILDING
F. C. CHIHUAHUA AL PACÍFICO

1872 Albert Kimsey Owen, one night in September on his first visit to Topolobampo Bay, rounded out his dream of a shorter rail route between the United States and a Pacific port, Topolobampo.

1881 In June, *Texas, Topolobampo and Pacific Railroad and Telegraph Company* was granted a concession by General Manuel Gonzales, President of Mexico, 1880-1884. Included concession for construction of a city at Topolobampo. Promptly laid out by Owen and named "Gonzales City," site chosen was the north side of the inner harbor.

1882 Concession enlarged in December to be a 99-year grant to build and operate a railway from Topolobampo across north Mexico to Piedras Negras, with a branch to Presidio del Norte, and another branch between Álamos, Sonora and Mazatlán, Sinaloa. Extension into United States to terminate at Fernandina, Florida or Brunswick, Georgia or Galveston, Texas.

1885 In February, railway construction began in the form of surveying, clearing and grading inland from the bay. Project languished due principally to Owen's preoccupation with his "cooperative colony," a socialist enterprise.

1887 May 10 concession granted to Luis Huller; included rights to build a railroad between Juarez, Corralitos and Magdalena.

1888 Owen proposed to the Kansas City Council the formation of the *Kansas City, Presidio del Norte and Topolobampo Railroad.*

1890 President Díaz supported the concession and subsidy promise previously granted. Financial support sought in London.

1891 In July, there was organized in Colorado a *Mexican Western Railroad Company.* This supplanted the British financing prospects.

1891 "In August 1891 . . . I left Topolobampo Harbor . . . traveled mainly along the route reported by Engineer Holbrook for the *Mexican Western Railroad Company* over the Sierra Madre to Chihuahua City, accompanied by Mr. E. H. A. Tays, Chief Engineer of the Company; Mr. Kneeland, photographer for Credit Foncier; Messrs. Thornton and Patrick — five Americans, a mozo, six riding animals, two pack mules, a local guide . . . Bayside to Chihuahua City is about 450 miles. Examination of the line was from Vegaton to Carichic, the latter about 130 miles west of Chihuahua City." Carichic is slightly east of the present railroad.

Southwestern Utopia, p. 94

1897 Concession was renewed.

1897 September 18 line completed between Juarez and Corralitos.

1897 Soon after above, *Río Grande, Sierra Madre y Pacífico* organized to operate the system.

1897 March — Enrique Creel and Alfred Spendlove purchased a portion of rights granted Call and Pacific Railroad in November 1894. This permitted them to build a single line from Chihuahua City to the coast of southern Sonora. (Basis of Chihuahua and Pacific)

1897 Survey started.

1898 March 25 construction started.

1898 April 13 *Chihuahua and Pacific Railroad Company* incorporated in New Jersey.

1899 "Reportedly negotiated with Enrique C. Creel, then vice-president of the projected *Chihuahua and Pacific Railway*, concerning an extension of the C. & P. to Topolobampo." *Owen.*

1899 July 15 the first C. & P. train left Chihuahua City and ran to end of track at Santa Isabel 33 miles west.

1900 May 20 the line opened between Chihuahua and Miñaca.

> 1900 Concession for extension of line by *Río Grande, Sierra Madre Pacífico*, cancelled for non-performance.

> 1907 Sold out to *Mexico Northwestern Railroad*, a British company.

1900 In 1900 Owen "interested Arthur E. Stilwell and a group of Kansas City bankers, held conferences with them, Governor Ahumada of Chihuahua and President Don Porfirio Díaz, which resulted in organization of the *Kansas, City, Mexico y Oriente Railway.*"

1900 On February 11, at a testimonial dinner at the Midland Hotel, Kansas City, Arthur Stilwell announced plans for a railroad from Kansas City to Point Stilwell on Topolobampo Bay. (Stilwell had recently lost control of the *Kansas City, Pittsburgh and Gulf;* founded smaller railroads.) Involved 1610 miles of railroad and would bring the Pacific 400 miles closer to Kansas City.

1900 On February 12, Stilwell met with Dr. Woods and Church White of the Bank of Commerce and laid the financial groundwork.

1900 Soon after Stilwell headed for Mexico. Visited Enrique C. Creel in Chihuahua, enlisted his aid; Creel joined forces bringing in the *Chihuahua and Pacific*, and as a result was made a vice-president of the *K. C., M. & O.*

1900 Soon after there was a meeting with President Porfirio Díaz and a concession was arranged. Construction was to proceed east and west from Chihuahua and east from Topolobampo.

> 1900 March, railroad completed between Chihuahua and Miñaca. *Chihuahua and Pacific Railroad Company.*

> 1900 August, relinquished concession to build to coast beyond Miñaca. (Possibly combined with Owen concession to terminate in Topolobampo.)

1900 *Kansas City, Mexico and Orient Railroad* was incorporated in Kansas on May 1. Subsequently its charter was legalized in Mexico.

1899 On July 15 the Panhandle and Gulf Railway was incorporated and was a revival of the unfinished *Colorado Valley Railroad Company* which had built 7 miles of track south from Sweetwater. The Panhandle and Gulf was to build between Sweetwater and San Angelo.

1900 On March 3 the old Panhandle and Gulf Railway Charter was amended to permit construction of a line between Red River and the Río Grande and the name was changed to the *Kansas City, Mexico and Orient Railroad Company of Texas*, a subsidiary of the *K. C., M. & O.*

1900 Financing from the Midwest was preferred by Stilwell. Kansas, Oklahoma, and Texas were enthusiastic. Towns and cities along the route contributed or invested substantial sums. There were some English investors as well.

1902 Grading began in Oklahoma and Mexico. Construction began in five sections:
  1. North and south from Milton, Kansas;
  2. North from Sweetwater, Texas;
  3. East from Chihuahua City;
  4. West from the Chihuahua and Pacific track end at Miñaca;
  5. Northeast from Topolobampo.

1902 In late March the first rail was laid in Mexico.

1903 On April 30 trains ran between Chihuahua and Trancas, 35 miles northeast.

1903 Three locomotives sent to Mexico in April and most of the line was located except the grade through the Sierra Madre not yet established. Ten or 15 tunnels planned in Mexico, all but one on the west slope, and two or three loops.

1903 Grades: 1½% east of Chihuahua; 1% in Fuerte Valley east from Topolobampo; 14% maximum for 40 miles of cog railway in Sierra Madre contemplated, but further surveying located a 5% grade line and later work located three routes with 2½%; final plan included grades up to 2½%.

1904 In December, 62 miles of road opened between Topolobampo and Fuerte.

  1904 Edmund A. Hovey, a scientist, mentions riding the new railroad, in winter, to its terminus at Nuevas Casas Grandes about 150 miles SW of El Paso. *Río Grande, Sierra Madre and Pacific Railway*.

  1904 A branch track existed between Miñaca and Temosachic.

  1904 Creel obtained concession to construct a line between El Carpio (La Junta) and Temosachic. *Chihuahua and Pacific*.

  1905 July, opened the line between El Carpio and Temosachic.

1905 Early in the year the rails completed between Miñaca and Sanchez 7 miles SW of Creel. From Sanchez at 8045 feet the western descent begins.

1908 Road completed between Trancas and Falomir, 84 miles NE of Chihuahua.

  1909 October 19, *Chihuahua and Pacific* sold their rights to the *Mexico Northwestern Railroad*, a British company which also had acquired the rights of the *Río Grande, Sierra Madre y Pacífico*.

  1909 October 19, purchased *Chihuahua and Pacific*. Short time before had acquired *Río Grande, Sierra Madre y Pacífico*.

  1909 November 22, consolidated their concessions into one (M. N.) and received additional authorization to build a road Madera to Juarez. Road rights completed between La Junta-Madera-Juarez.

23

1911 By March, *Mexico Northwestern* was the successor of the *Chihua-hua and Pacific* between Chihuahua and Miñaca.

1911 By March services varied from daily to tri-weekly.

1910 Stilwell would take prospective investors, particularly to the Creel Divi-
to sion in Mexico, the best built part of the system.
1912 Pancho Villa had been a contractor for building the railroad in western Chihuahua. Stilwell did not like him, which possibly influenced the revolution's impact on the railroad.

1910 The Revolution stopped construction in Mexico and the superintendent,
to Juan F. Treviño, fled to El Paso for the two years that Villa controlled
1912 Chihuahua.

1912 March 7, the financial difficulties of the *K. C., M. & O.* culminated in receivership and ousting of Arthur Stilwell.

1912 Of the 950.6 miles of railway received, the mountain section in Mexico was in good condition. Mostly 70-75-pound rail (60 in most of Mexico) spiked to untreated ties with little ballast.

1912 Unsettled political conditions precluded work on the 75 miles between Falomir and the Río Grande which, however, had been graded. Nor could work be done on the 200-mile gap through the mountain-barranca between Sanchez and La Junta, Sinaloa. This involved a drop of 7389 feet and costs were estimated as high as $500,000 per mile.

1915 June 30, receivers discharged.

1915 December 8, reorganization plan put into effect, and the new corporation was chartered as the *Kansas City, Mexico and Orient Railroad Company*, which absorbed the *Kansas City, Mexico and Orient Railroad* and other facilities. Mexican situation still too unstable to permit construction.

1917 April 16, the parent company went into receivership again, but the *Orient of Texas* was returned to its owners.

Following the new receivership, the *Mexico Pacific Division* struggled along and operated a tri-weekly mixed service in the Fuerte Valley when no revolutionary battles were being fought between Topolobampo and Fuerte.

Villa's revolutionaries and other armies were constantly tearing up the track between Falomir, Chihuahua, and Sanchez, so service was irregular.

1920
to The road came close to failing completely.
1923 A combination of forces saved the road. Involved were federal agencies, states, counties, towns and cities, labor, management and other railroads.

The Mexican lines which operated were self sustaining. But most of the track in the State of Chihuahua was out of operation.

The road was really saved by oil.

1922 Two tank cars of oil loaded at Fort Stockton.

1923 May 28, the Santa Rita well "blew in" at Big Lake. Oil prosperity in-creased general freight revenues.

1924 March 27, a partial reorganization in the form of a forced sale took place because the government foreclosed a loan which matured before the increased prosperity could retire it. The new operating company was called the *Kansas City, Mexico and Orient Railway Company*. Financial affairs, however, continued to be complex.

1924 Mexican government began aid to help restore the road there as partial repayment of damage due to the revolution. Seven carloads of rail reached Falomir; Conchos bridge opened and much other rehabilitation work completed.

1925 There was more money for everything – maintenance, etc. Advertising claimed $1,711 as against $4 in 1923.

1925 *Mexico Northwestern* connected with *K. C., M & O.* at Miñaca.

1925 Mountain Division restored.

1925 Between Creel and Miñaca, the connection with the *Mexico Northwestern* trains ran two or three times a week.

1926 Construction began on new line between Fuerte and San Pedro.

1927 By spring, mixed service twice weekly train running as far as Pulpito, 92 miles east from Chihuahua.

1927 Oil accounted for 48% of the road's income.

1928 In January, Congress authorized the bridging of the Río Grande near Presidio, Texas.

1928 September 24, Santa Fe Railway gained control of the *Kansas City, Mexico and Orient.*

1928 Before integration of the U. S. part of the system had begun, the *Santa Fe Railway* sold the three Mexican divisions to Benjamin F. Johnston and United Sugar Company of Los Mochis, Sinaloa. For $650,000 cash and mortgage of $900,000, Johnston received 316 miles of railway, 95 miles of it new, 16 locomotives and other equipment assigned to Mexico.

1928 Soon after Johnston purchased the Oriente, its operation was combined with the *Mexico Northwestern,* whose president, L. Roy Hoard, provided the management. Certain facilities consolidated.

1928 *Ferrocarril, Kansas City y Oriente, S.A.* became the new name of the Johnston railroad, the Mexican part of the system.

1928 Johnston and L. Roy Hoard, president of the *Mexican Northwestern*
to *Railway,* combined forces for administration and construction economics, specifically as a consequence of the depression. Operating terminal was moved to La Junta.

1930's Both companies stayed in business but neither made any money during the1930's.

1930 In October the first train rolled into Presidio as a consequence of completing the last gap in the system north of the border. The completion of the 1960-foot open pile trestle across the Río Grande made possible a traverse of the proposed system all the way to Creel, Chihuahua. The only rail gap to Topolobampo was 199 miles, Creel to San Pedro.

1937 In March, Benjamin F. Johnston died.

1939 Secretary of the Treasury of Mexico was authorized to open negotiations for purchase of the *Kansas City, Mexico y Oriente, S.A.*

1940 Transfer was made in the spring and included a settlement of the *Santa Fe Railway* mortgage.

Oriente operations were immediately separated from the *Northwestern* and Don Juan Treviño was reinstated as manager.

The La Junta-Miñaca branch of the *Mexico Northwestern* was purchased by the government. Miñaca lost its junction status and is now just a way station. La Junta Junction used jointly.

1940 Since then service mostly twice-weekly mixed each way with occasional tri-weekly motor car.

Lumber and mining traffic increased in the Creel division during the 1930's. A tri-weekly service Creel-La Junta. Seldom made the *Mexico Northwestern* connection at La Junta.

1940 Schedules over the Pacific Division, Topolobampo-San Pedro, various. Business reduced by road paving between Los Mochis and San Blas. Most traffic between Los Mochis and San Blas during peak agriculture season. Traffic between Los Mochis and Topolobampo slight.

In 1940's some refurbishing of the line occurred and talk began about closing the open link through the mountain.

1941 June 30, the parent *Kansas City, Mexico and Orient Railway Company* ceased to exist corporately as a consequence of a merger with the Santa Fe Railway.

1940 Began rehabilitation.

1940 Rehabilitated 88 kms.

1941 Rehabilitated 145 kms.

1941 Studied route along Septentrion.

1943 Surveyed route 140 kms. out of Miñaca and did some preliminary grading, Creel to Cuiteco.

1944 Established line between Sanchez and Pitorreal. Rehabilitation work between Creel and Sanchez. Access roads completed in region of Temoris.

1945 Work intensified in Mountain Division.

1946 Lumber and mining revenues increased over 1930's. *Mexico Northwestern.*

1946
& More rehabilitation and grading.
1947

1948 Eleven tunnels finished — totaling 908 meters.

1949 Grading completed between San Pedro and Topolobampo. Buildings constructed at San Blas.

1950 Construction work suspended; reconstruction continued.

1951
& Reconstruction work continued.
1952

1953 Construction work began again.

1954 Rehabilitation work on Topolobampo-San Pedro, Ojinaga-Chihuahua, La Junta-Juarez. Construction work only on grading and drainage.

1955 Construction of 53 kms. of grades and work on access roads. Relocated 170 kms. of access roads so as not to obstruct construction route.

1955 *Mexico Northwestern* merged with the *F. C. Chihuahua al Pacífico.*

1956 Continued work on drainage, bridges, access roads, etc.

1957 Intensified work: 6 tunnels, 6 bridges.
Reconstruction work Miñaca-Aldana.

1958 22 kms. of grade, 1500 meters of grade and drains, constructed 5 tunnels and 3 bridges, worked on foundations of 3 big bridges, 5 kms. of elastic roadbed between Aldana-Creel, rehabilitated 180 kms. of old road and put in operation.
Actual construction period.

Construction completed in 1961 — Creel-San Pedro, etc.

1960 Construction activity greatly accelerated, with tremendous activity in the Mountain Section; rail-laying began in the latter half of the year.

1961 Rail-laying put on a crash program because of the official opening scheduled for the latter part of the year.

1961 November 23, the President of Mexico with official guests from all over the world together with many representatives from the communications media, traveling by special trains, opened the new section and the system near Temoris.

Some Towns and Cities

OJINAGA

Presently, Ojinaga, Chihuahua is the eastern terminus of the F. C. Chihuahua al Pacífico. In the early history of this line (then known by other names), it was a relatively unimportant point on the system where it crossed the Rio Grande. Ojinaga is on the south side of the river, while Presidio is on the north side in Texas.

Since the river, except when in flood, offered but little inconvenience to communication between the two communities, their beginnings and histories have much in common. It is a convenience to consider Ojinaga-Presidio together. For now and again circumstances put relatively more importance upon being one side or the other of the Rio Grande, here the boundary between Mexico and the United States.

An early name for the south side of the present boundary was La Junta de Los Rios. Here is where the Rio Conchos flowed northeastward to join the Rio Grande. Its lower route made a natural way for earlier travelers among the Spanish explorers to approach the country and prospects beyond. The legendary treasure of the Cibola country was an early magnet. A copy of Cabeza de Vacas' *Narrative* was instrumental in reviving this interest.

It appeared in Santa Barbara near the headwaters of the Conchos, and an expedition was organized to investigate. But since royal ordinance forbade military expeditions as a consequence of the failure of Coronado, this one must have other sponsorship. It became a missionary venture in search of virgin land in which to convert "lost souls."

The year was 1581. Three Franciscan priests — Fray Augustín Rodríquez, Fray Francisco López, Fray Juan de Santa María — nine soldiers, 19 Indian servants, 600 head of cattle and 90 horses moved the easy way down the Rio Conchos drainage to the junction with the Rio Grande.

Here they found numerous Indian *rancherias* (villages) and placed crosses in several. The narrator of the expedition found the men handsome and the women beautiful. They appeared happy and carefree and lived in houses made of logs and brush plastered with mud. Corn, beans and squash were raised by not much corn. Farming was paramount.

These Indians, like many in Mexico, gave the padres much encouragement. They requested that priests be sent and built several chapels modeled on that of El Paso as evidences of their faith. So missionaries

27

finally were sent. On June 12, 1684, missions were formally established at La Junta de Los Rios on the banks of Alamito Creek.

Later on the Chihuahua Trail became a main freight route into Mexico and crossed the river at this point. Non-Latin settlers arrived in 1848. They built Fort Leaton as protection against the Indians in 1849 on the north bank.

Some years later Benito Juarez became president of Mexico. An important local supporter was Manuel Ojinaga. His services were rewarded. He was made a brigadier general August 4, 1865; then on October 23, 1865, by presidential decree, San Francisco de La Junta de Los Rios became Ojinaga.

The drama of this was more personal than communal. The community of the south bank was still but some hundreds of inhabitants living in a small town of adobe bricks. It was a desert situation of the type referred to by travelers as a small, dusty border town. Some mining was carried on in nearby hills and mountains; some farming was concentrated along the courses of the rivers.

The sun-baked tempo of life was here increased somewhat with the construction of the railroad in the early part of this century. Then came the revolution. During its turmoil, thousands of refugees fled through Ojinaga in 1913 and on across the river and border to the safety of Presidio on the north bank.

A more important event was the bridging for rail traffic of the Rio Grande authorized by the United States Congress in 1928. But later in the same year, the Santa Fe Railway sold the Mexico part of the Kansas City, Mexico and Orient to Benjamin F. Johnston. At one stroke, then, Ojinaga became the eastern terminus of a new railroad instead of an important border point on a transcontinental system still a-building.

Was a future blighted or a beginning made? No one can say with certainty. Ore is still taken from the hills and cotton and vegetables still grow near the rivers. With water, lots more would grow. And who knows what is under the soil.

The railroad has brought somewhat more activity to Ojinaga. There are more tourists who travel down the line, and more freight moves across the border. More of many things would bring changes to Ojinaga — more ore, more water, more freight. It has grown to be a slightly larger, sun-baked, dusty, desert, border town. But who can say what will be the effect back along the line when Topolobampo, the western terminus, becomes a port for all the Pacific world. Then, the conductor may be proud to roll on his tongue the call Ojinaga (O-HI-NÁ-GA, O-HI-NÁ-GA). For the F. C. *Chihuahua al Pacífico* is proof that dreams do come true.

West of Ojinaga. Ing. Francisco M. Togno photo.

CHIHUAHUA

Chihuahua City has been the promotional and administrative center of the *F. C. Chihuahua al Pacífico* for much of its history and is the present headquarters of the system. Geographically it is not quite central, being only 140 miles west of Ojinaga. Economically it is central and is a bustling city of north Mexico.

Chihuahua is a combination of two Tarahumara words said to mean "Place of Work" or "Place of the Workshop." The word has a pleasant explosive quality much used throughout Mexico for expressions of surprise, amazement, or admiration. Anyone who has not visited Mexico for ten years will have many occasions for such pleasant use of the word in the city itself.

Particularly in recent years, the State and City of Chihuahua have had the advantages of fine, progressive leadership. This city is but one of many which reflect the general progress.

A new modern water system was completed a few years ago, and piped throughout the city. The Colonial aqueduct, built in 1790, with its high arches, is essentially part of the local tour, although water still runs through it. No doubt it supplies water for some of the communities near the city. A friend of mine, an expatriate Chicagoan of forty years' record, is enthusiastic about the water from the new system, and is fond of boasting how much better it is than Chicago water, which often makes him sick. Eventually almost everything seems to come full cycle. Chihuahua!

All of the principal streets have recently been resurfaced and paved. This project carried with it the obligation, on the part of bordering property owners, to refurbish and paint. As is usual with taxes everywhere, this was done with considerable grumbling, but the result has been a source of pride. Chihuahua!

The parks department was given more funds for beautification. A number of places about the city received attention and contributed to the general fine effect. The most important effort was along the small stream which bisects the city. Much work has been completed, and only the addition of trees and flowers are necessary to make a delightful park of it. Chihuahua!

Speaking of beauty, I have yet to read an account of a Mexican city or town which did not claim to have the greatest feminine beauties of the country. And included was the evening when they, at least the young unmarried ones, could be found promenading around the plaza. There is no reason to make an exception of Chihuahua. I have been at the plaza a number of times, but have forgotten what day of the week it was when the promenade occurred. Chihuahua! Chihuahua!

The Tarahumaras were right, too, about it being a place of work. Activity is most notable in morning and evening, going to work and coming from work. There isn't a mad rush about it, but an air of pleasant bustle. The people are friendly and have a purpose — to make a living, to do a good job, and have some fun in life. So, although a reasonable amount of socializing goes on during the day, the evening is primarily devoted to the latter. What the tourist calls "night life," is not characteristic of this community. Chihuahua is rather a family town. Few people have the inclination just to seek pleasure; work is more satisfying.

The climate is conducive to work. It is delightful, in my opinion. The altitude is 4593 feet, average mean temperature for the year is 64°F. The extremes, of course, push into warm weather in the middle of summer, and some days around freezing in winter. Although the city was not located for its climate, it could have been.

A major feature of its economy is the mining industry. Mines are located in the suburbs, as is a big smelter. With these one finds many kinds of associated services. Cattle ranching and lumber are also very important businesses which center here, while the field activities, as it were, are many miles away in this big state, the largest of Mexico. Light industry is increasing too. Chihuahua is growing.

It is the capital of the state, so the government is located here. And there are many regional offices of the federal government located in Chihuahua. Some of the more notable buildings are for the offices of the city, state, and federal government.

The State Capitol Building was constructed in 1891 on the site of the Jesuit Colegio de Loreto. The latter was abandoned by the Jesuits in 1767 when they were compelled to leave Mexico, and it became a military hospital. Here the Father of Mexican Independence, Cura Miguel Hidalgo y Castillo was imprisoned and executed in 1811.

A more recent revolutionary figure in Mexican history is General Francisco Villa. His home, at the time of his assassination, La Quinta Luz, is at Calle 10, North No. 3014. This is a fifty-room mansion where his widow lives and maintains a museum of Villaiana: swords, pistols, uniforms, photographs, and the bullet-riddled Dodge touring car in which Pancho Villa was riding when killed. Señora Villa gives a very entertaining tour through her home, in Spanish or English.

On the northwest edge of town is the station of the *Mexican National Railway*, a notable building. Near it are the buildings and campus of the University of Chihuahua. Several thousand students attend here. The university is not completed, but is interesting to see while passing along. No doubt, a closer acquaintance with the facilities would be even more interesting.

Arts and crafts are not so characteristic of this city and region as they are in southern Mexico. A number of things are produced for the local market, but to my knowledge none have been listed as arts or crafts of the area. There are craftsmen, but these are servicemen rather than artists.

From crafts to the animal world in one short step brings us to the "Chihuahua Dog." This mite of vivacity weighs in at 14 ounces, or can reach two pounds. Such a specimen is *muy grande,* and not an everyday Chihuahua. This should caution you about purchasing a bargain on the street without his patent of ancestry. Some of these tiny creatures grow into monsters, whose appetites will give you a settled purpose in life.

The better residential areas are on the edge of town near Highway 45. There are a number of fine mansions supported by fortunes gained in the industries of mining, lumbering and ranching. Entrepreneurs in other fields have also done well, for Mexico offers fine opportunities to get ahead.

Several churches are notable, and are near the edge of the city. But the most imposing building is the cathedral on the central plaza. It is an excellent example of the baroque style of the Colonial Period. Building was started in 1717, but not completed until 1789. According to tradition, an inclined plane of earth was used as a kind of scaffolding, surrounding the rising structure. When the highest part, the 146-foot tower was completed, the ramp of earth had risen so as to bury the structure, and removal was necessary to reveal the beauty of the building. The interior no longer compares with the splendor of its former condition when enriched by fabulous gold and silver furnishings. The patron saint of the city is San Francisco de Asis, and the church is dedicated to him.

Chihuahua has a relatively short history as compared to many major Mexican cities. As is true for a good many communities, interest in the locality was concentrated by the discovery of ore. Please remember, a major impetus for the colonization of much of Mexico was a series of "gold rushes," successively pushing the frontier northward. In this case, the precious metal was silver, and was discovered about the end of the seventeenth century, possibly 1679. The settlement in connection with the mining was formally organized into a town in 1709, and was called El Real de San Francisco de Cuellar. In 1716 the town, through the official exertions of Don Juan Felipe de Orozco y Molina, was promoted to the status of a city, and called Villa de San Felipe of the mine, or Real de Chihuahua. A little judicious pruning did the rest.

For various reasons Chihuahua was not as disturbed as many similar places by the troubles of the times, and it quickly grew strong enough to endure and absorb what came its way.

So it has continued to grow and prosper. Now its population is in excess of 300,000 people, and the future gets brighter. It is headquarters for the *F. C. Chihuahua al Pacífico.* New buildings raise its skyline to impressive proportions. The inhabitants are looking forward to, and planning towards more visitors to their capital. It is a fine place to add to your travel itinerary, and a strong addition to your vocabulary. The word is Chihuahua! Chihuahua! Chihuahua!

SISOGUICHIC

One hundred seventy miles southwest of Chihuahua is Bocoyna which is a small village on the *F. C. Chihuahua al Pacífico*. It is the stop for Sisoguichic, fifteen miles east by a rough road. The latter community represents the largest concentration of Tarahumara Indians in the entire tribal area. Here too, is a concentration of good works among this tribe. How did all of this come about in such a remote spot?

A pleasant valley lies near the continental divide of the Sierra Madre Occidental in southwest Chihuahua. It is long and narrow, for it is near the headwaters of an upper branch of the Conchos River. This river takes a meandering course for many miles to the north and east and joins the Rio Grande, which in turn, after many more miles, flows into the Gulf of Mexico. So the cool waters of the Sierra flow across three-quarters of the widest part of Mexico before mingling with the tropic waters in the Gulf.

Before man came into this mountain valley (and no one knows when he came), it is likely that the meadow bordering the stream was greener and more narrow. The pines and oaks pushed towards the banks and perhaps some shaded the quiet pools, and flowering shrubs marked the sinuous course of the creek. More birds sang; more small animals scampered over the ground and through the trees.

Man came, cleared the trees from the low, rich land, planted crops, erected shelter, and stayed. This became home. But it is a valley home, not a concentrated community. Families spaced themselves at intervals of a quarter to a half mile on both sides of the stream for a distance of eight or ten miles. This was the method of settlement of the Tarahumara Indians, and is one of their strongest cultural traits even today. They were situated in this manner when the Jesuit fathers found them in the latter part of the seventeenth century.

The Jesuit fathers attempted to concentrate scattered people around church, school and shops, and to teach improved agricultural methods in order to make communities or missions possible. Such a beginning had been made by Father Antonio Orena, so that upon a visit by his superior Father Zapata in 1678, there were 179 Christians in what the padres called El Nombre de María Santísima. The Tarahumara name is Sisoguichic, and it is called so today.

Sisoguichic was the most isolated pueblo in the early Jesuit mission system, and nearly the most westerly. It is near the western edge of Tarahumara country. It is 7000 feet in altitude, 15 miles east of Bocoyna and 27 miles northeast of Creel, which is just over the continental divide.

A very significant occasion for this growing community was the day in March 1681, when Father Joseph Neumann arrived to become the resident missionary. To reach his charge he had traveled almost four months from Mexico City, and three years from Prague. He was delayed for two years when a fleet sailing from Spain was missed by a few hours. But the intervening time was well spent by Father Neumann in becoming proficient at a number of crafts soon to be useful in a one-man, do-it-yourself mission. There had been no time to learn the Tarahumara language. Nevertheless, Sisoguichic had been without a resident missionary for three years and was eager for another. It got a vigorous and devoted padre in Father Neumann. He was resident missionary for twenty years and its visitant for the following thirty-one. Moreover, he wrote a history about missionary work among the Tarahumaras, and this document is one of the most important sources of information about these unusual people.

Father Neumann was brought to his mission by Father Bernardo Rolandequi and the two priests were welcomed, when still some miles away, by a delegation of five Tarahumaras. They were led by the Indians, under arches of boughs, to a little church and a hut for the father. As it was Lent, and the Tarahumaras already knew flesh and fowl were not acceptable, the fathers were served a meal of eggs, beans and tortillas. After refreshment, Father Rolandequi exhorted the Tarahumaras regarding their duties to the new padre, picked up his walking staff and headed for Carichic, 30 miles northwest.

Father Neumann then proceeded to undertake a half century of service among the Tarahumaras. For their part, the Indians were diligent. A new church was already under construction. It was finished in 3 weeks. In another 3 weeks the Indians had finished the padre's new house. The church was "christened, so to speak" by its first mass on Easter, 1681. Two head of cattle (of a 30-head herd) were killed for a feast, and this endeared Father Neumann to the Tarahumaras.

In earliest days: "I devoted myself to the instruction of the children. Twice daily I gathered them into the church. In the morning after Mass, I repeated with them the *Pater Noster,* the *Ave Maria,* the *Credo,* the precepts of the *Decalogue,* the sacraments of the church, and the rudiments of the Christian doctrine. I had brought these with me in a translation into the Tarahumara tongue, and I repeated them from the written text. In the evening, I reviewed the lesson, and also asked the children questions from the catechism. At the same time, I gave instruction to those among them who were still pagan, acquainting them with the principal mysteries of the Faith, and preparing them to receive baptism. The rest of the day was spent visiting the sick and hearing confessions — although, to be sure, I heard but few — or in assisting the builders and directing their operations. For in these countries the fathers themselves are the only architects, and the Indians are the only masons." Father Neumann also did carpentry, cabinet making, and was his own "cook and steward, tailor and launderer, sacristan, and nurse for the sick — in a word, everything."

These labors were hard, but rewarding. There were problems too, some not of local origin. Soon after Father Neumann arrived, he was warned to be watchful about trouble from the west. Carosia, a pagan *cacique* (chief) of the Guazapar tribe, was agitating against the mission program in the upper Mayo River country. Considerable harm was done there, but in 1685 Carosia's people turned against him and he fled to the vicinity of Sisoguichic. He was arrested, but for crimes he did not commit. Father Neumann defended him successfully and won his release from the Spanish officials who had apprehended him. As a consequence, Carosia, the robber, rebel and murderer, was converted together with his family, and he was christened with the name Dionysius. This man was representative of Father Neumann's major problem: opposition by the local *hechiceros* (variously referred to as witches, sorcerers, medicine men). The christianizing, civilizing, and farming programs of the fathers reduced the influence of these local leaders and chiefs. The most successful programs first won over the leaders.

Other serious problems came with the colonizers who frequently followed the fathers. They moved progressively northward, lured by gold, silver, and other mining strikes, and by the rich farming and grazing lands which thereby came to their notice. Here was wealth, but labor was needed to secure it. The local Indians were commonly impressed to supply the labor, even against the protestations of the padres. There were other injustices, some simply due to lack of communication. Even the padres made some mistakes and were rebuked by their superiors.

A somewhat minor trial, as Neumann said a number of times, was the Tarahumara's love of their scattered existence, and hence the difficulty of bringing them to pueblo life. This they would endure for a while, and then take to the hills, a form of escape in which many still indulge.

More serious was the fact that certain diseases, particularly smallpox and measles, came with the Europeans and devastated the Indians. There was a plague in 1693 and another in 1695. Both carried off many lives in Sisoguichic. The *hechiceros* said the sound of the church bells provoked the plague and that baptism spread it. And there were signs to confirm that "evil spirits" were abroad in 1696. An earthquake occurred in April, and a comet appeared in October, the sun was eclipsed, and other "supernatural" events took place.

Thus many factors combined towards a serious general revolt among the Tarahumaras in 1697. A number of missions were destroyed and several fathers were martyred. Sisoguichic was destroyed about June 25, 1697 — the church, houses, huts, and crops. Shortly thereafter, soldiers and loyal Tarahumaras fought and killed many rebels. Peace was restored the following spring.

The church was rebuilt in 1702 by Neumann who was still the spiritual administrator, although he had been transferred to Carichic a short time before. It is interesting to note how much of the existing stone structure goes back to this date.

After the great uprising, a good many missions were rebuilt better than before, and the work prospered in spiritual and secular ways. More conversions were made and more churchly affairs were turned over to the Tarahumaras. Neumann's records tell us that 24 pueblos remained untouched and that one-half of the Tarahumaras had not revolted. They prospered too, as farmers and herders, and their churches reflected it.

The Bishop of Durango made a visit to many Tarahumara missions in 1717. By that time, many boys had been taught to read and write Spanish, and to play musical instruments. At a ceremony at the mission of San Francisco Satevo, the Bishop was delighted by the skill of the neophytes who assisted and intoned the chants and other songs. And there was an orchestra with flageolets, bassoons, violins, harps, and an organ. The choirmaster was a Tarahumara.

Father Neumann then passed the last twenty years of his missionary work in tranquility, and completed his great history in 1724. He composed its dedication in Carichic on April 25 of that year. This most valiant and able of all of the fathers among the Tarahumaras died May 1, 1732.

But the work continued. An official visit of the missions was made by Father Guendulain in 1725. Another was made by Father Ignacio Lizasoain in 1761. At Sisoguichic in 1725 there were 280 families, 290 cattle, 308 mules and burros. In 1761 there were 140 families, 620 cattle, 67 horses and mules. There was an even greater reduction in the population at some of the other missions. In this connection, Father Lizasoain reported: "It appears the Tarahumara missions have passed their prime." But in 1746, twenty-two missions, mostly in the southwest area, had been handed over to the care of the diocesan clergy. They no longer needed active resident missionaries. More Jesuits could be spared for pushing the work northward.

It was but a short time, however, before the crushing blow fell. On June 24, 1767, royal orders were opened by the Viceroy of New Spain under prescribed official conditions. All Jesuits were to be expelled from New Spain. By July 27 all Jesuit missionaries to the Tarahumaras had been assembled and were forced to leave Chihuahua. Some days later they met the Franciscans traveling north to take over "their" places at the pueblos.

There is less detail about Sisoguichic's story for the next century and a quarter. Perhaps here is appropriate use for the expression: "Its life pursued the even tenure of its ways." There were some minor ups and downs, but a general continuity in the pattern prevailed. So there was a solid foundation for the future when the Jesuits carried through plans for reinstituting their work.

In 1903 a catechism in the Tarahumara language was prepared. A house for the care of orphans was established in 1904 by the Institute of the Servants of the Sacred Heart of Jesus and of the Poor. Sisoguichic was elected to have one of four boarding schools, primarily for children and orphans, established by the Jesuits in 1905. A new and greater period of active good works had begun.

It has been my privilege, and that of my companions, to visit this community several times since 1957. We camped a few miles away in a scenic spot near a small waterfall. From here we joined the life of the community: we watched the children in school and at play; observed the teaching of crafts; took part in the religious festivals; heard the grinding of corn and smelled the tantalizing aroma of tortillas toasting for hungry, but sturdy and sparkling-eyed young boys and girls; visited the new hospital and marveled at the serene, smiling acceptance by these active people, of the quiet regimen required to combat tuberculosis; watched a sawmill carriage move back and forth for the cutting of a soft whitish mineral deposit into building blocks, which later hardened into stone; heard about the radio education program that would transmit lessons to former students, who carried receiving sets back to isolated groups many miles away; and became aware through these various avenues of perception as reflected by Fathers, Sisters, boys, girls, general community, that we were in an aura of sympathy, kindness, and just plain goodness.

Sisoguichic is in a dynamic phase. The hospital is new, and more dormitories for boys and girls at the school are abuilding. It merits a visit, however rough the road. Certainly the people of Sisoguichic and their programs deserve support.

CUITECO

Estación Cuiteco came with the building of the *F. C. Chihuahua al Pacífico*. It is approximately 237 miles southwest of Chihuahua City and on the west slope of the Sierra Madre Occidental. This is still high rugged country and was difficult to reach until recent years. Nevertheless the early padres came into the region, built a church, and a community was established around it. This old village is about a mile from the station.

By the time of Jesuit missionary activity in Mexico, it had become a very common occurrence for Indians to send delegations to an already established mission, to request that a Father come and establish a new mission among them. Many benefits were derived from such a new mission. Tools and techniques, many different kinds of crafts, new and improved agricultural methods, and an interest in music and musical instruments, were observed to add greater security and interest to the lives of those tribes who had them. Also, many tribes formerly at war with each other, lived more at peace. This was a matter of great consideration even among the most war-like of the tribes having an agriculture-centered culture. Moreover, the religious message and observances brought by the Fathers had a ready acceptance among many tribes. The degree of acceptance varied in proportion to the degree of enmity of these peripheral nomadic groups. The deviations from this attitude of acceptance came from tribes which were essentially hunters, gatherers, wanderers and raiders.

Before the seventeenth century, the Tarahumaras were frequently in conflict with their neighbors to the south, the Tepehuanes. Because of this enmity, a considerable territory between them had become too risky for settled use by either group. The heart of this area was a fertile river valley, the Valle de San Pablo. Indian delegations requested aid in bringing this area into peaceful use. Father Juan Fonte visited it in 1607, and established a mission at San Pablo Balleza by 1610. Of course everything did not go smoothly from these beginnings. There were problems, some quite serious. But the civilizing process had begun, and would spread in a similar way to the north and west.

These missionary processes were sometimes preceded by secular activities of mining, ranching, colonizing, military expeditions and so on; at other times they were concurrent; and in many remote areas lacking any significant material attraction, secular penetration has been very slight until recent times. Into this latter category falls the town of Cuiteco, which was about equally remote from the Sinaloa-Sonora activity to the west, and the Tarahumara missionary program to the east. But the church got there.

Cuiteco has an altitude of about 6000 feet. Formidable canyon walls are both above and below its location, so in terms of accessibility, it occupies an intermediate situation in the barranca country. It is near the headwaters of the Septentrion River. The immediate area has a kind of openness in a rough, precipitous terrain. There is no flatness, no stream-side meadows worth the name. The nearby hills are rolling and farmable. The horticulturist would recognize it as good country for orchards, and so it is.

The most notable agricultural products are apples and apricots, both very delicious. Some of the local people make homemade brandy from their apples. Those who have sipped it, rate it with the best *calvados* or apple jack.

On a rail tour in 1964, a few of our group were invited to join a family gathering seated in the terrace garden before their home, over-looking Cuiteco and the surrounding mountains. The soft spring air, the flower-scented breeze, dusk and evening sky about the hills, the friendly but desultory conversation suitable to our limited vocabularies, and the mellowing effect of *calvados* Cuiteco, combined into a mood now felt as the "Cuiteco mood." Whatever the heat of the day might bring, dusk in such a pleasant environment is always a time of peace and contentment.

It is equally charming at other times of day. Wander about, turn, and look all around. In almost any direction your gaze finds a picture. It is fine and satisfying country, and wonderfully pleasing to the man with the eye of an artist or photographer.

The cottages and homes are often amazingly aesthetic in their form, proportion, and texture. Not big and fine, but inviting, and somehow just right for their location and inhabitants.

The people are very modest, but welcome the opportunity to be friendly. They think of themselves as poor. None are affluent in material things, only in the intangible quality of happiness. Their riches are not easy to assess, but evident to the sympathetic heart.

There is a church now in process of restoration. The original structure dates back to the late seventeenth century. Construction already completed, consists of adobe brick walls with surfaces plastered, and a roof of wooden beams and shingles. The apse has been rebuilt of solid stone masonry, and has stained glass windows. The work is also progressing on other parts of the building, but it will probably take a good many years for the economy of these people to complete the rebuilding.

Once, when we were at the church, we found a padre in temporary residence. He had come for a short visit to hold services and look after the spiritual needs of the community, which was not large enough to support a resident priest. Cuiteco is a *visita* of a church administrative district. This same practice was carried on in earlier days when the early Jesuit activity in the north was administered from Durango. Under the district were several missions, one being the mission of San Joaquin y Santa Ana, of which Sisoquichic was a *partido*. After a while Cuiteco was attached to Sisoguichic as a *visita*, and became part of the charge of the resident missionary, who visited at intervals, and performed services in the church now being restored.

Next to the church is a school, and beside the school is a small store. Another small shop is diagonally across the street from the church. This should give the reader an idea of the size of old Cuiteco, which has a population of several hundred people.

New Cuiteco is about a half mile downstream, or farther along the railroad. The new town came with the railroad, as did easier communication. Until a few years before active engineering began on the railroad, Cuiteco's access to the outside world was only by trail — horse, mule, burro, and foot.

When construction, grading, and bridging began for the railroad, a worker's camp was built. This is now New Cuiteco, and the station is here. Also, there is a school, several stores, and a number of cement and stone houses. The people who live here are mainly railroad employees, who in various capacities, help to keep the railroad operating. They come mostly from elsewhere, and there are several hundred of them. Nevertheless, they fit in well with the older community.

So the trains come and go. There used to be several each week. Now there are several each day. Still, the life of these communities remains about the same. Of course, the number of trains will increase, and change will occur. Our train stops for a night several times a year, and shares a movie or a visit with the local people.

Do outsiders come often to Cuiteco? Probably very few. I recall a man we met once, who invited us to a visit in a garden in Old Cuiteco. He spoke some English, and was a businessman who had come to the peace of Cuiteco from the bustle of Los Mochis. Here he could sit among the flowers under the evening sky, sip *calvados* Cuiteco, and watch the trains go by.

And what did the hoarse diesel horns say? Perhaps they said, "Mañana, mañana."

EL FUERTE

El Fuerte is three miles from its *F. C. Chihuahua al Pacífico* station, but is building towards it. It is at the edge of the maritime plain, 342 miles southwest of Chihuahua, but in the state of Sinaloa. In the sixteenth century it was important because of its strategic position on communication lines. A note of interest is that this early role of importance, because it was located on the El Camino Real, will be given new emphasis by the completion of the railroad. For history and tourism often go together.

The "Road to Cibola" was already long in use by 1564, when Francisco de Ibarra decreed the erection of a frontier villa called San Juan de Carapoa, or de Sinaloa. The original villa may have been where the town of El Fuerte now stands, or else a few miles downstream at Bajada del Monte. Subsequent destruction and rebuilding may have resulted in a slight shift of location, which may never be exactly known. Even so, the founding of present El Fuerte is given as of that time and place, and the local people celebrated the 400th anniversary of the community in 1964.

A short time after the villa was established, it was destroyed. The reaction to the depredations and other cruelties of the de Guzmans continued for a good many years, and some of the settlements had turbulent beginnings. The settlement here on the Fuerte River was one of them. But eventually the good works of the padres won the confidence of the Indians, and the Spaniards consolidated their colonizing efforts northward.

El Camino Real became the established route of colonization and communication, and San Juan de Carapoa became a strong point along the way. The name was changed to El Fuerte because of a fort built on a low hill at the edge of the river. A portion of the old structure has been modified to serve as a reservoir for the town water supply. So the idea of "beating swords into plowshares" does come true on occasion.

Mining was carried on in this region in the old days, and still is today. The search for precious metal was a principal incentive for the early colonizing efforts of the Spaniards.

However, the Fuerte River Valley was a fertile agricultural area before the conquerors came. Much of it was dry farming, with use of irrigation where possible. Here the banks of the Fuerte were too high, however, for the limited engineering skill of the Indians. Large-scale irrigation development had to wait for the development of more modern techniques.

El Fuerte has had a prosperous history, but in a less spectacular way than Alamos. There are quite a number of relics from the colonial past, some fine mansions, the stone church, and the plaza, which they border. Essentially, the town has a colonial atmosphere.

The town is laid out in a fairly regular way, unlike a good many Mexican towns of like size. A very charming feature is that the streets are surfaced with small cobblestones laid in patterns. These have a smoothness not commonly associated with cobblestone construction. The principal streets are bordered by trees. There are about 15,000 inhabitants.

Perhaps the most important phase of El Fuerte's history occurred while it served as the capital of the State of Sinaloa. But this was years ago. The capital is now Culicán.

El Fuerte is in the midst of the great irrigation project for the Fuerte Valley; the dam is about eleven miles upstream, and most of the irrigated fields are a good many miles downstream. No doubt, the immediate area around the town will receive a larger share of this productive water in the future. The present slight development may be because the land in the near vicinity is less level, and not as suitable for irrigation. Nevertheless, downstream from the town there is a long, narrow strip of rich farm land, a major factor in the economy of the region. But dry farming occurs in suitable spots all over the surrounding area.

The Miguel Hidalgo Dam, across the Fuerte River about eleven miles upstream, is one of Mexico's biggest. Behind it is a lake, backed up for thirty miles, with a maximum width of twelve miles. This offers good catfish and carp fishing, the people say. Such being the case, these waters need a restocking program to supply more productive and gamier fish. Such a program would yield more fish for the table of the local people, and attract more sports fishermen.

There are plans for greater development of the recreational potential in this water resource. Perhaps you will soon see Indians with headdresses streaming about their ears while skimming down the lake on water skis.

In the meantime, El Fuerte is a delightfully quiet town to visit and to saunter around. Modest accommodations are available. The *F. C. Chihuahua al Pacífico* station is a few miles from the town, so there is no train noise to distract. More recently, the access road to Highway 15 has been paved. This will bring in more people. And when the El Camino Real connecting with Alamos is refurbished, many motorists traveling north or south will be bound to take in this historical, scenic loop: Navojoa-Alamos-El Fuerte-Los Mochis. Many will be charmed to stop along the way.

If you belong to the school which values and collects the "backwater" places with a tempo and appeal of their own, plan to come soon. El Fuerte may never be so quiet again.

LOS MOCHIS

Los Mochis is twenty kilometers from the western end of the *F. C. Chihuahua al Pacífico,* twelve miles from the sea. It is a booming city of over 140,000 inhabitants, and was founded in 1903 by Benjamin F. Johnston, an American citizen. Johnston was active in the planning layout of the city which was established in support of a large sugar refinery he had built there.

The refinery was conveniently located among vast sugar cane plantations controlled by Johnston. These prospered and Los Mochis grew. An interesting sidelight is that the irrigation works, in part developed by the cooperative group brought to the area by Albert Kimsey Owen, in due time became a part of the Johnston plantation complex.

The plantations flourished, the refinery became the largest sugar producer in Mexico, and Benjamin F. Johnston became a major financial power in that part of Mexico.

His interests eventually came into conflict with the Mexico branch of the *Southern Pacific.* This railroad controlled much of the transport from the sugar refinery at Los Mochis. There was disagreement about rates, and Johnston cast about for other means of moving his sugar. This led to another interesting sidelight — the purchase in 1928 from the *Santa Fe Railway* by the Johnston interests of the Mexican divisions of the Kansas City, Mexico and Orient. But since Johnston died in 1937, he did not live to see any of his sugar products hauled over the *F. C. Chihuahua al Pacífico.*

Certainly the name Los Mochis as popularly understood does not reflect the vigor of Johnston nor of the present community. In native Indian dialect it is "Place of Land Turtles." But there is nothing tortoise-like about Los Mochis. It is bustling even during the hot weather of summer, not only the finest growing season for cane and corn, but best for deep sea fishing nearby.

Presently it is the financial, economic and industrial center of the El Fuerte Valley. Here is Mexico's largest irrigation potential, not yet fully developed but booming, The damming of the Rio Fuerte, miles above, has brought not only power but tremendous agricultural development. Besides cane and corn, rice, wheat, cotton, tomatoes, cantaloupes, watermellons and vegetables are grown and shipped to the United States and Canada. And its full potential is not realized as yet.

Many thousands of acres of rich land await the coming of water to bring forth waving fields of grain and vegetables. This is dependent upon the extension of the irrigation project even beyond the present plan. The water is available. And Los Mochis is preparing for much more expansion. Not the least element in the plan is a fine water system which the local Chamber of Commerce boasts as being "one of Mexico's most modern purification plants."

Parque Sinaloa is an outstanding botanical garden which came to the city from the Johnston estate. It is a fine tourist attraction, although much more could be made of it. Mr. Johnston collected plants, flowers and trees from all parts of the world and surrounded his residence with them in attractive combinations of lawns and gardens. The house has become a ruin. The lawns and gardens, in part, are maintained but not developed. Much could be done to bring out the botanical significance of the garden. But Parque Sinaloa is a delightful and flowering place most of the year.

Sportsmen have been coming to Los Mochis for years, since it is central to outstanding fishing and hunting. A fishing calendar which applies has been listed under Topolobampo. A hunting calendar follows:

Nov. 1 to Jan. 25	Goose	Speckled
Nov. 1 to Feb. 25	Duck	Pintail, sprig, canvasback
Jan. to Dec.	Dove	White wing
(Aug. & Sept.)		(peak dove shooting months)

Inquiry will also develop other hunting opportunities.

The Hotel Santa Anita is a good center for sporting activity since the same management operates the Yacht Club of Topolobampo. It is a common sight to see sportsmen in the dining room feasting on their take of the day. Arrangements for hunting and fishing can also be made through other local hotels — Beltrans, Hidalgo, Figueroa, Del Valle — and Motel Chapman. And tourist facilities are expanding. To be up-to-date on available facilities and information, the reader can inquire of the Chamber of Commerce, Apartado Postal No. 66, Los Mochis, Sinaloa, Mexico, and receive a reply in English.

Los Mochis is about 3 paved miles west of Highway 15, a major route between the border at Nogales and Mexico City. It has a paved landing field, 1050-meters long, which is equipped for night landings. Not only is it easy to reach by car, plane or bus, the transportation picture is completed by being on the railroad. Here are found the shops and administrative offices of the Western Division of the *F. C. Chihuahua al Pacífico*. By one way or another, drop by, won't you! You will find a warm welcome in Los Mochis.

TOPOLOBAMPO

Topolobampo is now the western terminus of a completed railroad from Ojinaga to the sea. What was it like here when about a hundred years ago this system was just a dream? Listen to this piece of on-the-spot reporting written seventeen years after the occasion. It is not too difficult to separate the facts from fantasy. Both have and are still playing their part. And perhaps, developing facts may even exceed the fantasy: "IN 'TOPOLOBAMPO — A REMINISCENCE,' printed in the *Credit Foncier of Sinaloa,* issue of Feb. 15, 1889, Albert Kimsey Owen wrote:

I recall the occasion as though it were yesterday; one evening in September (1872) myself and my companion (Fred G. Fitch, engineer) came on horseback, at the close of a beautiful twilight, upon some Indian fishers encamped among the bushes on the west shore of Ohuira Bay.

Some giant pitahaya (cactus) trees stood nearby. Under one of these we unsaddled. A fire of dried cactus was blazing. A dozen dogs, a goat or two, some sheep, two women, three men, an urchin and a few milch cows . . . fish were hanging from the mesquite trees. The flesh of the green sea turtle, cut in strips, was dangling from the arms of the echos. (Giant cactus; more branched than the Sahuaro of the Southwest.) Many shells of turtles were lying around. Some served for seats, others held salt and fish. One was used for a cradle.

We were tired. Within a few minutes we were stretched on our blankets near the fire. I fell asleep. It may have been near midnight I awakened — fire smouldering — the moon had climbed above the mountains, and had thrown a soft light upon the camp.

An Indian came through the bushes from the beach with a turtle on his shoulder — let it fall to the ground — it flopped violently. He turned it on its back — it was quiet. He put a fish upon the live coals, seated himself upon a turtle shell, turned the fish once, and when it was brown and steaming, he took off skin and scales as one skins an eel, and thus prepared, he ate it.

After this, he placed a peccary skin over the breast plate of a turtle, threw himself on top of both, and with a turtle shell for a pillow and his feet upon a sleeping dog he was, in a few minutes afterward, breathing heavily.

I had traveled many days through the wilderness and over swollen rivers (500 miles from Mazatlan during the rainy season) in search for this out of the way and but little known bay. My curiosity was keen to see the water and to investigate my surroundings. I stole from my blankets, went through the bushes and looked. What a panorama — there was Ohuira — an inland sea!

Mountains rose directly from out the water to the east and south. Ripples played on the edge of the incoming tide, and a dugout canoe was lying far up on the shore . . . to the north and east stretched a level plain of grass and chaparral.

Thought I, if the morning should discover a deep and safe channel from this inland sea to the Gulf of California, then here is the site for a great metropolitan city. On that water, now without a sail, will one day come the ships of every nation. On this plain will dwell happy families. The Australasian will crowd this shore to be welcomed by the European, who shall come by train from the Atlantic seaboard, over the plateaux and across the Sierras.

As I stood and afterwards strolled along the beach, these thoughts grew into fancies. I pictured the shipping lying at anchor, saw the flags of many nations, heard the striking of the city clocks, was attracted by the chimes as they played "Sweet Home" from the tower of the Normal Industrial School, looked at the stone quays shaded by tropical plants and flowers, listened to the birds singing within the courts of Spanish-Moorish houses — and only awakened from my trance after the dawn had tinged the eastern horizon.

Everything we examined combined to impress us with the importance of these Straits and Bays for a safe, deep and extensive anchorage. I settled that from that time on I would never rest until "Topolobampo" became a "household" word among commercial people, until the Republics of North America had utilized its advantages and Topolobampo had become a favorite place for the exchange of trade between the peoples of the world." (*A Southwestern Utopia,* by Thomas A. Robertson, The Ward Ritchie Press: Los Angeles, 1964, p. 26 ff.)

The next thirteen years brought little change in the scenes Owen saw. It wasn't until 1885 that a small party worked near Topolobampo cutting and surveying a line for the railroad. Then on November 10, 1886 the first group of a cooperative colony, another major Owen project, sailed into the Bay of Ohuira and landed near the camp of the railroad survey party. Other colonists soon followed, and thus began the development of Topolobampo.

This development was given much more impetus by the beginning of railroad construction in 1902, and still more when 62 miles of railroad between Fuerte and Topolobampo were opened in 1904.

Growth followed these improvements; not spectacular but steady growth. Communications made possible the establishment of a fishing industry, and canning of sea products followed. A town grew to service these industries, for the waters here are rich in produce of the sea. In fact, sportsmen are increasingly drawn to the area for deep sea and other superb fishing. Here is a valuable calendar of fishing opportunity:

Jan. to March — Sierra, currina, toro, yellowtail, grouper, cabrilla, skipjack, totuara, snook begins (El Fuerte River Estuary), pompano, roosterfish.

April to July — Currina, red snapper, cabrilla, yellowtail, grouper, dolphinfish, roosterfish, snook (in El Fuerte River Estuary), pompano, sailfish and marlin begin.

Aug. to Oct. — Currina, red snapper, cabrilla, marlin, sailfish, yellowtail, grouper, dolphin-fish, totuara, roosterfish, skipjack begin.

Nov. & Dec. — Sierra, currina, toro, pompano, yellowtail, grouper, cabrilla, totuara, skipjack.

The world's yellowtail record was established here. And the many estuaries provide oysters, scallops, butter clams, crabs, etc. for picnics on the beach.

There are miles of fine sandy beaches, clear water for skin diving and islands which provide permanent breeding grounds for water birds. So recreational opportunities in season are varied and outstanding. Tourist facilities are not yet numerous, but are developing. The yacht club is a good example.

Sea traffic is increasing also, going beyond local fishing industry. As the rail facilities are increased, the government is expanding the harbor facilities to produce a rounded transportation complex. So an expansion along all of these and associated lines is to be expected for Topolobampo.

Presently it is about four thousand in population. It may not become the metropolis visualized by Owen, but it is bound to become a prosperous city. It has a superb natural harbor, rich sea life, and booming agriculture on the maritime plain to the east. The traffic these will feed and draw is bound to be extensive.

Topolobampo.

ALAMOS

Alamos is not on the *F. C. Chihuahua al Pacífico,* but is within its sphere of influence. As access is improved, many passengers on the railroad are bound to visit it by reason of its outstanding historical interest.

Such access is only a matter of a short time because the members of the communities of Alamos and El Fuerte recognize that they have tourist attractions which can be made mutually advantageous. El Fuerte is on the railroad as well as on the old El Camino Real with Alamos about 45 miles away. Improve the road for bus travel and many more people will make this scenic and historical trip. This modern project is presently being pushed along. But what about its background?

When man afoot regularly travels considerable distances, he usually takes the easiest way. Such a way led northward, following closely the inner edge of the smooth coastal plain which borders the west slopes of the Sierra Madre Occidental. The Indians used this way, and through continued use, established it firmly. Professor Carl Sauer has called it the Road to Cibola. Later it was known as El Camino Real. Presently some of it is a back country road, little used. In other parts, it is but a track, overgrown by vegetation. Some sections are quite difficult to locate. A plan is maturing to restore portions of the route to provide better communications, as well as an interesting route to travel.

Introducing this route, Professor Sauer says:

In the New World, the routes of the great explorations usually have become historic highways, and thus has been forged a link connecting the distant past with the modern present. For the explorers followed main trails beaten by many generations of Indian travel. There was, in varying degrees, inter-communication and exchange of goods between Indian villages or tribes. The resultant trails were as direct as the terrain, the need of food and drink en route, and reasonable security permitted, and were fixed by long experience as the best way of traversing a particular stretch of country. Explorers, being sensible men if their explorations succeeded, used Indian guides who took them over Indian roads. By and large, European colonization still found these routes useful. Men on horses had the same need of saving distance, of finding easy passes and stream crossings, and of food and drink, that directed the Indians' travel afoot. Footpaths and packtrails rarely differ. Only as the whiteman brought new economic interests, such as the search for mines, and mechanized transport such as railroads, did he break away from the primitive routes of communication. Even then there has been a large measure of survival of the earlier historic and prehistoric highways.

Since this was written, the west coast highway has been constructed and paved thirty or more miles to the west, and the *F. C. Chihuahua al Pacífico* bisects the route at right angles. The qualifying conditions of new economic interests have been met.

In the early colonial days, much of the exploration to the north, particularly the search for the Seven Cities of Cibola, followed this route, hence the name. Among the earliest explorers, there was one expedition which camped among the cottonwoods along the Alamos River at its junction with the Guirocoba Arroyo. This event has been considered the beginning of Alamos, but among local historians there is considerable difference of opinion as to the identity and date of the encampment of this expedition. One said, "here in 1541 Coronado's army camped," and another stated, "it served as a campsite for Coronado's explorers in 1531," and a third gave the view that "Nuño de Guzman camped here in 1531." Professor Sauer wrote that Nuño de Guzman sent an exploration party under Diego de Guzman, which camped there in 1533. If a few years and individuals are important to the reader in this matter, my advice is to follow Professor Sauer. The charm of present-day Alamos will be little affected, whichever account is preferred.

The area, of course, was inhabited by Indians, and the Guzman camp may have been in conjunction with a village. It is questionable whether such a village would have survived the Guzman visit. Coronado and his lieutenants were notorious for their cruelty. The Guzmans in particular did so much slave raiding, pillaging, and burning, that many square miles of country were laid waste. In a few years they caused more ill will towards the Spaniards than subsequent colonizers could counteract. Much of the trouble with the west coast Indians in following decades has been attributed by historians to hatred and suspicion aroused by the Guzmans. At any rate, little is known about Alamos for a century and a half, except that missionaries were there in the early part of the seventeenth century. A major part of this story took place lower on the river, and went even beyond Alamos into the mountains to Chinipas and remote Cuiteco.

Then one of the richest silver mines of northwest Mexico was discovered near Alamos in 1684. This brought a good many Spaniards into the area, and attracted Indians from the missions lower on the Mayo River. In the usual colonial way, the Indians provided most of the labor for the mine.

Silver mining developed to a point that it won for Alamos the title: "Silver Capital of the World." Certainly it became very rich, and developed a population said to have reached 30,000 inhabitants, including the laborers working the mines and smelters in the vicinity.

49

One consequence of this mining activity was to denude the slopes of Mt. Alamos, and the country for miles around, of timber to support the mine tunnels and to fire the furnaces of the smelters. A similar result occurred in many parts of colonial Mexico since the search for gold and other metal, and the development of mines, was a principle activity of the Spanish colonizers.

Another consequence was the erection of fine mansions in Alamos by those who gained most from the mines. These were built so well during the several periods of prosperity, that they survived (at least in restorable form) several periods of decline as a result of rebellion and revolution. Riches attract envy too.

It is said that the youngest building in Alamos is a hundred years old. This is so because of the rich history of building, followed by more modern developments and communications farther away. El Camino Real was no longer the major artery of traffic. The descendants of the earlier builders lived in their isolated town as it decreased in population and its colonial glory slowly crumbled away. The mines were lost, closed or exhausted. Alamos had another phase of hibernation, as it were.

Then the purity of its colonial charm attracted the attention of the federal government, and it was declared a national monument. Modernization is not allowed — it can only be restored to conform to the colonial style.

An increasing number of prosperous Mexicans and *norteamericanos* have discovered Alamos, have come to retire and live in one of the old mansions, which they have restored. This is a major activity there.

Perhaps "activity" is too strong a term. For example, in the middle fifties when I "camped" on the Hacienda property and operated some pack trips into the back country and up Mt. Alamos, a scouting trip to a new area was in prospect. A number of the residents showed enthusiasm and expressed a desire to go along. A date was promptly set and they were invited. Nothing further was heard until the day before the trip when I circulated to learn the cause. Various weak excuses were given, but one person finally revealed the attitude of all. On being pressed, he admitted to being still very much interested, but just couldn't go. "You know," he said, "I guess I am just too busy doing nothing." This is the tempo of life in Alamos.

It is not a place for the tranquilizer set. And don't be misled by the claim that it is "the jumping bean capital of the world." This seed has a larva inside. When the larva moves, the bean gives a slight nervous twitch. This may be the most regular activity in Alamos.

So when you are there on a fine day, and you feel like a little jaunt, you can visit Aduana several miles away where the smelting and mining community was, or is. (A Canadian company is now mining the old tailings.)

Or, closer in, is the small Indian village of Uvalama where pottery is made by hand. I obtained a splendid movie of pottery making, as well as many still photos, but this requires time, many visits, and somewhat more activity.

By all means visit the cemetery on the edge of town. This is so close that you can visit it on the way to your late morning beer. Here you can find the graves of two brothers who died in the revolution. They fought on opposite sides but both were heroes. And there are other things to do, but watch the activity, and don't get out of character with the town.

Another easy and very rewarding stroll is to the branch of the National Museum of Popular Arts and Crafts.

Two hotels in Alamos are operated by American management. The Los Portales is on the square, and in a fine old colonial mansion. The Casa de los Tesoros is about two blocks southwest from the square and in a large mansion, very charmingly restored. On several occasions the management has attempted to introduce the production of Mexican arts and crafts, and may have succeeded by the next visit. At any rate, the effort has culminated in one of Mexico's most interesting shops.

So Alamos is at present living, charmingly and comfortably, in the shadow of the past. It is now easy of access, but not on the *F. C. Chihuahua al Pacífico*. Still it is close enough, and interesting enough, to leave the line for a visit. When El Camino Real is restored between El Fuerte and Alamos, it will be a historical and scenic trip to take a bus from El Fuerte for a visit. In fact, this will be so short and easy that it will not flurry the tempo of life in Alamos.

CASAS GRANDES

The two *Casas Grandes*, the Old and the New, are four miles apart. To visit the Old by the *F. C. Chihuahua al Pacífico*, you must stop at the New, for the Old is now an archaeological site and a national monument. To make the visit, you travel the Madera Division of the railroad which makes a northerly loop between La Junta and Juarez. This was operated as the *Mexico Northwestern Railroad* for a good many years before it was absorbed by the existing system in 1955. Strictly speaking, the Madera Division loop is not a "main line" part of the *F. C. Chihuahua al Pacífico*, but is important and scenic and will become more traveled. Two good reasons are the settlements just mentioned and now to be described.

Old Casas Grandes fooled the experts. For many decades it was considered, by specialists from both sides of the border, to be an extension to the south of the comparatively well-known Pueblo culture of the Southwest, particularly the older form of it. And this, in spite of the observations and predictions, in the 1880's, of the famous archaeologist A. F. Bandelier, that it probably had an important mixed history and should be excavated at once. Of course it is such a huge archaeological site, over 237 acres, that it discouraged all but an organization which could command large resources.

Such an organization came into being. Three hundred thousand dollars were required, as well as highly skilled archaeologists. A combination of Mexican and U. S. institutions and personnel grasped the challenge, and began work in October 1958. Four intensive campaigns have been completed, and although the studies and definitive publication have not yet appeared as of early 1966, they are expected soon.

The cultural artifacts removed, of course stay with Mexico, the country of origin. This is a policy which is increasingly widespread throughout the archaeological world. As a result, persons or students who wish to examine the Casas Grandes material go to one place, Mexico City, and not a half dozen places scattered about the world.

What is the story for the general reader? Here is a rough outline:

1. *Pit house people*, the first known settlers, sometime between 700 and 1000 A.D. They had stone tools, red-on-brown pottery, random burials, relied heavily on hunting, but had farming. They came from the north from the Mogollon culture centered in west-central New Mexico and east-central Arizona.

2. *Anasazis,* pueblo-builders, were the next people to settle. They also came from the north where the homeland since the beginning of Christian times has been the "Four Corners" region of Arizona-New Mexico-Colorado-Utah. The chief characteristics of Anasazi are: farming, multi-storied house complexes; kivas; sand-painting; priestly offices; elaborate rituals and symbolism; special public dances performed by kachinas; corrugated grayish cooking pottery; decorated black on white or gray background pottery; decorated polychrome and glazed pottery. At Casas Grandes these people had an elaborate system of irrigation. Present day descendants of the Anasazis are the Hopis, Zunis, and the Pueblo Indians of the Rio Grande Valley.

3. *Mesoamerican people,* who moved in around the fourteenth century and lived side by side with the Pueblos until the town was next abandoned. They came from the south. Characteristics of their culture are: stone buildings; trade between north and south — metal objects from the south, turquoise from the north; elaborate ceremonialism, associated with pyramids and ball courts and possibly even human sacrifice.

4. *A Suma or Opata Indian village* (one of the problems to unravel), which vanquished the Pueblo-Mesoamericans shortly before 1565.

These latter people had their smaller village in conjunction with the larger Pueblo ruins surrounding them. The Spanish chroniclers, as early as the sixteenth century, were greatly impressed by the large size of the ruins, and referred to them as Casas Grandes. The name has stuck.

A mission was built near the Pueblo ruins in the late 1660's, mainly for converts among the Suma tribe. The mission's official name was San Antonio de Casas Grandes. Many Spanish settlers of the Rio Grande Valley fled to this mission when, after 1680, the Pueblo Indians revolted and drove them out. Their stay was short. The Sumas, with help from the Jaros and Jacomes, revolted in turn, and drove the Spanish still farther south. Not all of them survived.

San Antonio de Casas Grandes was burned, and some sixty people were killed. One of the gruesome results of the excavations was the discovery of the desiccated remains of at least forty individuals in one sealed room of the church.

Another incident of historical importance occurred here in recent times. A deep hole had been dug for treasure in the middle of one of the mounds associated with the site. Eighty casualties were thrown into this hole at the time of the Madero Revolution. They lost their lives in 1912 during the Battle of Casas Grandes. After the excavations are completed, the Mexican Government plans to erect a memorial commemorating these heroes.

Old Casas Grandes proved a good place to live, and may never have been unoccupied for long. When the excavators wanted to begin work in 1958, eleven families lived in the ancient rooms of the Pueblos. They grumbled when obliged to move several miles to modern houses of adobe bricks provided for them. They thought the old puddled adobe structures more comfortable.

But now that these historical treasures have been discovered, Old Casas Grandes has achieved a new status. It has been declared a national monument, and guards patrol it day and night to prevent vandalism. A program of reconstruction is in progress. Here is another known treasure of Mexico's rich archaeological past. It will be preserved and made available for students and interested travelers, both from home and abroad.

What of Nuevos Casas Grandes? Here is one area where it is no historical problem to distinguish the new from the old. They are four miles apart.

When the railroad (*Río Grande, Sierra Madre y Pacífico*) was completed in 1897, to Corralitos, and extended a few years later to Pearson, it bypassed the old site. Nuevos Casas Grandes sprang up four miles away. It is a prosperous, growing town of a good many thousand inhabitants.

The immediate area is dairy and farm land. The soil of the valley is fertile and has attracted immigrants. Many Mormons settled there in the late nineteenth century. A good many of them left with the revolution and fighting of 1910-1912. However, a good many stayed or returned, and have several thriving colonies, or colonias, near Nuevos Casas Grandes.

A principal reason for the railroad was the mining industry, located mainly in the mountains to the west. Here, also, are important timber resources and associated lumbering activities. The *F. C. Chihuahua al Pacífico,* Madera Section, is pushing ahead with reconstruction to service this traffic. The improvement is bound to attract more passenger use on the part of out-of-country travelers. For not only will Old Casas Grandes draw the tourist; there is much fine scenery in the mountainous country beyond.

CIUDAD JUAREZ

Ciudad Juarez is the northern terminus of the *F. C. Chihuahua al Pacífico,* but this has been true only since 1955. At that time the *Mexico Northwestern* was absorbed or merged. The Madera Division of this system was not a part of the main development of the parent system, but the La Junta-Chihuahua Division was. In effect, to get part, was to take all. Moreover, the future has an important part to play for the Madera Division, and it is well to acquaint ourselves with this northern terminus.

Ciudad Juarez usually is known simply as Juarez. It is the largest city on the United States and Mexican border and has a population in excess of a half million inhabitants. Opposite to it, across the Rio Grande, is El Paso, Texas. Since Juarez is a principal port of entry into Mexico, the border is a lively place, particularly mornings and evenings during the week. At these times there is a considerable exchange of local people between these cities. Apparently a good many live in one place and work in the other.

This suggests that their histories and development have much in common. This is true, although there is also a considerable difference between them. One writer has said that the Mexicans of this north country are "far less Indianist and traditional in outlook, custom, and manners than their kinsmen farther south. To a great extent, their cultural ties are much closer to the United States and the mores of the Rio Grande border country." The city is said to have an interesting Mexican-American atmosphere. You can hear almost as much English spoken in the streets as Spanish. Conversely, it could be said that El Paso has an interesting American-Mexican atmosphere, and almost as much Spanish as English is heard in the streets.

So it is that in this part of the country there is not that difference in art and custom that draws the traveler to southern Mexico. Not much in the way of arts and crafts is produced here, although great amounts are sold here, since Juarez has scores of shops and liquor stores to attract the shopper. Juarez can be a port of entry to more distant places of interest in Mexico, or can be a meager introduction for those not so fortunate as to be traveling farther.

One aspect of Spanish-Mexican culture which, in season, regularly draws many visitors is the bull fight. The Plaza de Toros Monumental is a handsome bullring, 3½ miles from the center of town, thus with adequate parking space. It seats 10,000 and offers fights each Sunday every month of the year except January, February, and March. Occasionally there are additional benefit fights, and some unusual cards of fighters are offered. Some preparation before a first visit is advisable.

Read a few books by writers such as Hemingway and Conrad. Then experience can add to your sociological education or get you on the way to becoming an *aficionado*.

The pre-Columbian history of northern Mexico, the Rio Grande River country, describes it as a kind of no-man's-land between Indian tribes. There was considerable trading, wandering and fighting back and forth. In between, there was not too much to draw settled occupation.

The country is 3000-4000 feet in altitude, and gradually increases in elevation toward the south. It is essentially basin and range country, a tableland with isolated small mountains, and a continuation of similar conditions in southern Arizona and New Mexico. The climate is temperate. Some snow falls in the winter and freezing weather occurs. The summer months are warm to hot. Sunshine is usual for most days of the year, which suggests little rainfall. It is semi-arid desert country with some grass among the sparsely situated cacti, yucca, agave, mesquite and creosote bush. Agriculture and irrigation was possible for the early farmers mainly along the Rio Grande and other streams where there were narrow strips of fertile soil.

The Spaniards came with horses and great changes followed soon afterwards. In the sixteenth century, Coronado and other explorers traveled north. Many of them went through the most natural break in the terrain, which they called Paso del Norte. When the Apaches and Comanches got horses they returned the visit, and sometimes raided as far south as San Luís Potosí and Zacatecas. "Early in the nineteenth century hordes of Apaches and Comanches poured across the Mexican border from the U. S. to winter, like troublesome tourists, in the balmy climate of Chihuahua and Coahuila."

Then along came the travelers of the Santa Fe trail, and some continued farther into Mexico to Chihuahua and beyond. What a mixed group of Indians, padres, Spanish conquerors, armies, businessmen, bandits, women and children went through this pass!

To control it was to control the route of easiest access into Central Mexico. It was a natural place for a stronghold and a town. In the early days it was not always strong enough to hold its own. But the location was sound; time passed, and now two large cities are located here in the Paso del Norte. One retains, in part, the name — El Paso.

Interestingly, Ciudad Juarez was founded in 1662 as Paso del Norte, but the name was later changed to Juarez in 1888. It was a temporary capital of Mexico when President Benito Juarez moved the seat of government there in 1866, during the intervention of Maximilian and the French.

The most interesting historical building is the well-preserved Mision de Nuestra Señora de Guadalupe, which was built in 1659 by Father García. Its adobe walls are four feet thick. The hand-carved wooden stairway, beams, and altar are regarded as marvels of workmanship.

There are two notable local fiestas. The fiesta of Santa Barbara occurs on December 4, and that of San Lorenzo on August 10. The latter is in the nearby village of San Lorenzo and although the fiesta actually extends from August 8 to 12, the 10th is the most interesting day. The Indian matachina dancers are particularly fine. There is an interesting tradition about this fiesta, which has always been a very popular event in the area.

"During the colonial epoch a statue of San Lorenzo (Saint Lawrence) was always carried from Chihuahua City to San Antonio, Texas, to celebrate the anniversary of the saint. The village of San Lorenzo was an important rest-stop for the pilgrims. Once, while making the stop, the Rio Grande flooded, preventing the march from continuing. The people took it as a sign that the Saint preferred to stay in the village. A chapel, and later, a church was built to house the image."

Juarez, to keep in step with other parts of Mexico, has a big renovating and improvement program. This is most apparent at the border crossing. New and much larger facilities are being constructed on both sides of the border to expedite the increased travel between the countries. Other public and private works continue to spruce up the city. So Juarez is making it more attractive for the tourist to tarry awhile, instead of rushing through to the south.

The most important event in Juarez' recent history was the border incident of the Chalmizal Strip. This, for a change, was a pleasant international incident, which drew the Presidents of Mexico and the United States to celebrate the successful conclusion of the problem in late 1964. The difficulty was caused by the Rio Grande River, which is the boundary between Mexico and the United States at Juarez-El Paso.

Some years ago, at a time of flood water, the Rio Grande left its boundary course and moved over into Mexico for a short distance and thereby put some Mexican land north of this fluid boundary. By the former treaty this had become United States territory since it was north of the Rio Grande. The Mexican owners and the Government of Mexico felt differently and claimed it for their own. It was a reasonable claim, and was resolved on the basis of the former course of the river. The treaty was amended to make this possible, and the celebration commemorated this happy example of internation good will. It is hoped that this presages the beginning of policies as fluid as the Rio Grande, and far more considerate. For, certainly, a river should not be allowed to come between friends.

Tarahumaras can get as far as Ciudad Juarez.

Natural History Notes

The major emphasis of this outline concerns the western two-thirds of the region served by the *Chihuahua al Pacífico Railroad*. This is considerable country. Its features are tremendously varied; many are quite dramatic. Access has not been easy, so penetration by the student or the scientific investigator has been limited.

Not many years have passed since the scientist, launching upon an investigation, could say it was with the prospect of traversing virgin territory. If one reduces this region to areas, it is likely that much untrammeled country is still to be found. Here is much material for theses, and challenging work for the established scholar. The rumors are of rich finds by the few who have come. Not all of this material is published, and the sum of it would not make a complete picture. It may be quite a few years before the synthesizer can produce a competent general work. Nevertheless, a few notes will supply some information, stimulate interest, and suggest broader investigation.

PHYSIOGRAPHY

The border country of Mexico-United States, in the vicinity of the continental divide, is a region of small isolated mountain ranges surrounded by plateaus. The impression often is of a mountainous condition. Actually the plateau area is greater than that of the mountains.

Continue to the south and a consolidation of mountains occurs. In less than one hundred miles, these have become a range known as the Sierra Madre Occidental. Its crest forms the boundary between the states of Sonora and Sinaloa on the west, Chihuahua and Durango on the east.

Generally speaking, drainage to the east is over gradual slopes and many miles. The principal rivers are the Conchos and Rio Grande. The higher plateaus grade into the plains and lower areas of the river valleys, until eventually the gulf receives the waters at sea level. For the most part, the gradient is gentle, water flow sluggish, and its cutting and carrying power weak.

In the higher plateau area there is also a minor but significant phenomenon. These are basins, not unlike those in other arid and semi-arid regions. Their drainage is local and inland, and not connected with main seaward drainage systems. From the moderately higher peripheral areas, drainage flows towards the lower parts and accumulates centrally as a shallow lake without an outlet in some basins. At other times, the streams involved diminish, until they disappear from seepage and evaporation.

To the west, however, drainage is more abrupt. From the crests, the slopes fall away acutely. Escarpments are common for many miles in certain areas. Since the slopes have a high angle, streams of the drainage are swift and have great cutting and carrying power. As a consequence, great canyons have been cut in the western section of the range.

Moreover, the conditions of altitude and slope make for a proliferation of upper tributary streams which cut the west side into a maze of ridges and canyons. These factors are further accentuated by the fact that these higher altitudes draw the heaviest precipitation. Hence, each major stream has its major barranca, some the equal in depth to the Grand Canyon of the Colorado. It may prove to be that some of the larger subsidiary streams have canyons which are even deeper. Adequate surveys have yet to be made.

The principal western streams are the Río Sonora, Río Yaqui, Río Mayo, Río Fuerte, Río de Sinaloa, and Río Culiacán. The order is from north to south.

The superior power of these western streams, particularly branches of the Río Yaqui, has resulted in encroachment into the former eastern drainage area. Gradually these headwaters capture, for their own, areas formerly draining to the east. And so it is that in such regions, the continental divide is now a good many miles east of the actual crest.

The student of geological forms calls these major landscape features "the plateau and barranca sections of the Sierra Madre Occidental province."

The next major feature to the west is a province of parallel ranges and valleys, a belt about 55-75 miles wide, trending a little west of north.

Beyond this is the Sonoran desert province. A typical area is the arid region from the foothills to the Gulf of California, on the latitudes between Guaymas and Hermosillo. A first impression is of mountainous terrain, but closer observation shows that it is primarily a plains region.

To the south, along the coast, is another major form feature, the coastal plain. It has been formed by the convergence of the deltas of the Yaqui, Mayo, and Fuerte Rivers. Since large agricultural irrigation developments are centered here, great sections of the coastal plain are well marked by vast fields of sugar cane, wheat, cotton, tomatoes, etc.

The person with a discerning eye who travels over the *Chihuahua al Pacífico Railroad* system and to the north over the *F. C. Pacífico*, may distinguish most of these features with ease. The most difficult to spot would be the province of parallel ranges and valleys. Still there is evidence of these features at El Fuerte, and this can be even more easily seen by a visit to Alamos from Navojoa.

So much for the major topographical characteristics. Scattered within the same general area are numerous features of a geologic nature. Their degree of importance may be relative, that is, they may be minor because of small effects, or because of present lack of knowledge of the scope of occurrence. Further investigation will undoubtedly require re-evaluation of a good many elements in the geologic picture.

Certainly this region of the railroad exhibits most forms of geologic action, some of them in dramatic style. Folding, upthrust faulting, faulting and tilting, emergence and subsidence, deposition, overthrust, and even some evidence to suggest vast underlying batholiths, have been noted. Aside from various examples of igneous intrusion, the most prominent evidence is of igneous extrusion. Great floods of lava, in numerous successive flows to a depth of several thousand feet, have covered earlier deposits.

In the mountain-barranca country, the streams in their lower courses have cut into very early material which needs further study for close identification. In this region are folded sedimentary rocks and some igneous materials, some of which are much changed and metamorphosed. Above is a considerable thickness of folded cretaceous rocks, both sedimentary and volcanic. These surfaces were covered in Tertiary times by several thousand feet of volcanic material. So in general, the upper 2000-3000 feet of rock showing at Divisadero is volcanic. Possibly less than half is older folded rock, much of which is sedimentary.

The major features then, of the country in northwest Mexico, traversed or skirted by the railroads, are great plateaus and deep barrancas. The plateaus average about 6500 feet in altitude, with a gently rolling surface, higher portions, and occasional peak-like masses rising to about 9000-10,000 feet. The barrancas on the west side are numerous and tremendous. Five thousand feet of depth is certainly quite common. A few places of greatest contrast have shown depths of 6600 feet. These figures suggest the spectacular quality of the views to be seen here. It is to be expected that further work will reveal many more items of information to astonish the curious, and also bring to attention new views to enthrall the traveler.

One more geologic fact will interest the rail fan. Along the coast, differential warping has occurred. Some sections of shore line have risen, others have sunk. One important area of submergence resulted in Topolobampo Bay, which made it a fine natural harbor and the choice western terminus of the *F. C. Chihuahua al Pacífico*. Here it is that rail traffic from the Midwest can now reach a harbor on the Gulf of California, and thus the vast Pacific world.

CLIMATE

There is almost more talk of the weather these days than in early times, when most of the population farmed or gardened. Every radio and TV station mentions it several times a day. As a consequence, factors which affect climate are increasingly common knowledge. One factor which is important is the face of the land, its configuration, its physical features, whether it is high, low, flat or mountainous.

The states of Chihuahua, Sonora, and Sinaloa have one physiographic feature in common — the mountainous Sierra Madre Occidental. Each has a more important feature which is but little shared. Chihuahua is mostly Central Plateau which is no part of the other two states. Sonora is mostly Sonoran Desert, but it shares some Coastal Plain, which is a major feature of Sinaloa.

The *F. C. Chihuahua al Pacífico* serves important parts of these states, but physically just misses Sonora in the southeast and northeast.

If you were to take a map of Northwest Mexico showing the major physical features mentioned, and super-imposed a map of annual rainfall, you would notice, broadly speaking, that precipitation follows rather closely the elevations of the land. The higher areas have more rainfall than the lower. There are deviations, true, but there are explanations for these. ¿No es verdad? Usually there are, when a general theory is locally applied.

There is more rainfall along the north coast of Sinaloa than on most of the coast of Sonora.

Temperature is another climatic condition affected by altitude. The area belongs in the temperate zone if subject to winter frost, to the tropical if frost free.

Another map will show that most of Sinaloa and some of Southern Sonora is frost-free or tropical. These are areas of southern latitude and low altitude. Notable exceptions are fingers of the tropical region which reach up into the great barrancas. Here the effects of altitude are countered by the protection, absorption and reflection of the canyon walls. Here the banana fronds blow, and flocks of green parrots give their winging cry.

Average Precipitation (mm)

	January	February	March	April	May	June	July	August	September	October	November	December	Annual Mean	Length of record (yrs.)
Bocoyna	30.6	26.2	23.2	11.6	4.3	77.4	209.6	193.0	71.0	37.2	16.6	36.1	706.4	5
La Junta	30.4	6.9	7.7	9.4	0.7	27.3	142.1	110.7	48.1	26.4	4.7	8.3	416.2	8
Guerrero	7.8	12.9	3.8	4.7	12.9	41.9	137.9	162.3	55.3	25.5	20.4	28.7	514.3	15
Temosachic	8.6	5.1	8.4	5.3	10.7	25.3	113.4	130.0	68.7	29.0	15.3	37.2	457.0	10
Madera	23.7	20.0	1.6	8.7	13.9	4.9	66.7	77.7	28.7	27.8	8.5	37.0	319.2	3
Cuauhtemoc	3.4	7.2	10.0	6.2	13.7	39.4	128.2	166.5	58.5	32.4	11.1	14.3	491.3	8
Chihuahua	6.1	5.5	5.9	4.4	7.2	34.4	80.2	122.9	87.7	23.5	12.0	10.2	400.0	19
San Buenaventura	2.3	2.5	3.6	3.5	13.3	5.7	109.6	103.8	25.3	36.2	14.0	28.9	340.7	4
Chinipas													721.0	

Average Temperature (°C)

	January	February	March	April	May	June	July	August	September	October	November	December	Annual Mean	Length of record (yrs.)
La Junta	8.4	11.0	12.1	19.9	18.2	23.1	23.3	22.7	21.7	18.3	12.7	9.2	16.6	8
Chihuahua	10.3	11.9	16.0	18.5	23.1	26.0	24.8	24.1	22.0	18.0	13.3	10.3	18.2	10
Cuauhtemoc	...	0.8	10.7	...	10.2	13.4	12.5	11.8	...	7.4	4.8	...	8.9	1
Guerrero	6.4	7.1	11.1	12.9	15.8	20.5	19.5	18.6	16.8	14.6	9.2	9.1	13.5	8
Temosachic	5.5	7.3	10.2	12.3	16.2	20.7	22.0	21.0	17.8	11.1	7.4	5.4	13.2	12
Madera	7.2	7.4	13.3	12.9	15.1	17.3	17.6	15.9	15.4	12.3	8.6	6.5	12.5	3

Pennington, Campbell W.—The Tarahumar of Mexico, U. of Utah Press, Salt Lake City, Utah, 1963, p. 27ff.

Total Precipitation (mm) Mean Figures

	January	February	March	April	May	June	July	August	September	October	November	December	Annual Mean
Alamos, Sonora	39.3	16.7	7.7	1.7	0.8	34.7	172.7	172.7	92.5	47.7	10.2	41.9	638.6
Obregon, Sonora	14.1	4.0	3.5	1.1	0.2	6.8	79.2	84.9	58.9	21.9	5.6	20.8	301.0
El Fuerte, Sinaloa	25.8	11.0	4.6	2.0	1.4	32.4	167.1	166.5	101.9	41.3	11.2	34.1	599.3
Guaymas, Sonora	12.1	5.8	3.5	1.6	0.9	2.0	45.5	66.7	50.2	18.6	7.8	20.5	235.2
Hermosillo, Sonora	12.9	7.8	3.9	2.3	1.0	5.4	59.5	79.0	31.3	16.7	7.7	16.7	244.2
Los Mochis, Sinaloa	17.1	4.3	2.9	0.8	0.4	8.5	49.2	83.0	80.7	41.4	6.3	17.0	311.6
Navajoa, Sonora	18.6	5.4	3.5	2.3	1.3	14.4	87.5	102.5	77.8	29.6	7.6	32.6	383.1
Nogales, Sonora	23.5	30.4	20.4	13.0	6.1	16.7	101.7	115.4	44.0	16.6	6.9	36.5	441.2
Topolobampo, Sinaloa	8.9	3.1	3.0	0.0	0.5	3.8	24.5	45.7	92.9	21.9	9.9	16.6	230.8

Average Temperatures (°C) Mean Figures

	January	February	March	April	May	June	July	August	September	October	November	December	Annual Mean
Alamos, Sonora, 389 meters	16.6	18.0	20.2	23.4	27.0	30.2	29.0	27.5	27.5	25.1	20.6	17.4	23.5
Obregon, Sonora, 51 meters	17.6	18.6	20.9	24.2	27.5	31.0	32.7	32.0	31.7	28.5	22.8	19.3	25.6
El Fuerte, Sinaloa, 100 meters	17.5	18.9	21.1	24.1	27.5	31.4	31.6	30.7	30.3	27.7	22.8	18.8	25.2
Guaymas, Sonora, 8 meters	18.0	19.0	20.8	23.4	26.3	29.5	31.1	31.0	30.6	27.1	22.7	19.3	25.0
Hermosillo, Son, 211 meters	17.3	19.1	21.0	23.9	27.1	31.2	32.5	31.8	30.9	27.7	21.7	18.0	25.2
Los Mochis, Sin., 15 meters	18.1	18.5	20.8	23.9	26.6	29.9	31.5	31.2	30.5	28.0	22.8	19.4	25.1
Navajoa, Sonora, 38 meters	17.8	18.8	20.7	23.3	26.6	30.3	32.4	31.8	31.0	27.9	22.8	19.3	25.2
Nogales, Sonora, 1117 meters	8.8	10.0	13.2	16.5	20.4	24.1	27.0	25.9	23.9	19.6	13.0	9.9	17.7
Topolobampo, Sin, 10 meters	18.1	19.0	19.9	22.3	25.3	28.3	29.3	29.3	28.9	27.2	23.6	20.2	24.3

Hastings, James Rodney and Humphrey, Robert R. edited by – Climatological Data and Statistics for Sonora and Northern Sinaloa, Technical Reports on the Meteorology and Climatology of Arid Regions, No. 19, July 1, 1969, U. of Arizona, Tucson.

At this point, you are invited to look at the tables of precipitation and temperature. Notice that the high places have more rain than the low places. Chinipas is an exception, since it isn't so high.

The high places are cooler than the low places too. If not, there are explanations. Consider Cuauhtemoc. It is shown to be higher than Chihuahua, lower than Madera, and colder than either. What is the reason? The rainfall was measured for eight years, and the temperature for part of a year. Unfortunately, data for two of the warmer months was missed. Of course, this threw off all the calculations, so we must wait for more data. Mañana, mañana!

The greatest recorded rainfall at Bocoyna was two and a half inches on September 23, 1955. On our last truck and trail trip, in the spring of 1960, all of the culverts were washed out for many miles in this high plateau country. We learned of a great rainstorm when we finally reached a town. Some people there told of how they were riding the train, which continued to proceed through water a foot or two above the tracks, while all the passengers were on their knees holding a prayer meeting for their safe arrival. And this was no laughing matter, and won't be for at least another ten years. Where this rain fell, I don't know. It just goes to show the records have not yet caught up. Moreover, during February, 1966, there was snowfall, off and on, for five days, the heaviest in the memory of anyone. But it is too early to know about these. Data must be hung awhile to be at its best.

The nub of the matter is, that there is seasonal precipitation. The rainy months are July and August; the driest, February and March. But now and again, there are some surprises in between.

When it rains, the streams rise, and are often in flood in July, August and September. These high waters can cause problems for the railroad. Motor vehicles, and other traffic over the roads, come to a halt until the water subsides.

Pennington says, "All of southwestern Chihuahua is distinguished by rather clear days throughout the year, except in summer when there are thunderstorms, which are frequently accompanied by severe hailstorms."

Temperature-wise, the hottest month is July, and the coldest, December. Generally, the lower altitudes are hotter and the higher cooler, so visits can be planned accordingly. Where there is moderate elevation and a greater range of temperature, the dryness of the atmosphere reduces the discomfiture. On the coast, there is the sea breeze to cool the bather. In the mountains, even during the warm days of summer, the nights require that coats and blankets be used to be entirely comfortable.

So the climate of this region is rather mild without real extremes. At its worst, it is tolerable; at its best it is delightful.

Note: Records of meteorological data are not adequate for an account of climate along the entire *F. C. Chihuahua al Pacífico* system.

VEGETATION

"Can you beat that?" said my traveling companion with excitement as he stared out the Pullman window of an *F. C. Chihuahua al Pacífico* passenger train some miles west of Ojinaga. "Aren't those Tarahumara Indians running toward the east? I thought their home country was several hundred miles west in the mountain-barranca region." "They certainly look and dress like Tarahumaras," I replied, "and you are correct about their homeland. But for centuries they have been coming to the vicinity of Ojinaga to gather *peyote,* a species of cactus used in some of their ceremonies. Before the coming of the Spaniards, they did not have so far to travel, but they are such strong runners that the greater distance is no serious problem."

The train continued its passage through the eastern part of Chihuahua. For the most part this is desert country. This does not imply a barren waste, however. There is considerable vegetation, except for the closed basins subject to seasonal flooding. Cacti and yucca are dominant but are interspersed with various shrubs and grasses. The creosote bush is characteristic in the most arid parts.

As the train moved farther westward, we noticed that a mesquite-grassland complex dominates the eastern base of the Sierra Madre Occidental and much of central Chihuahua. Some parts are characterized by almost continuous sods of grama grasses. Other areas have the grasses interspersed with shrubs and low trees, the most prevalent being mesquite.

The engine chugs upwards 125 miles west of Chihuahua City and reaches the mountain uplands. Here is a pine-oak forest, with some grass cover, and occasional meadows. Some of the latter are undoubtedly due in part to agriculture, as are many scattered fields. This is an important region for the economy of Mexico, and is also the most important for game animals.

The visitor with botanical interests soon notices a number of interesting oaks, and quickly asks what they are. It is not surprising that an answer is seldom given; there are already listed 112 species of oaks for Mexico.

As far as the average individual is concerned, much the same condition exists for the pines. Twenty years ago, 39 species had been listed, and this is enough to confuse the amateur and make the expert work.

In this pine-oak forest complex, there is considerable cover of grasses and other trees, shrubs, and forbs.

The boreal zone, in its lower aspects, is represented on some of the higher ridges and peaks of the Sierra Madre Occidental. Many fir trees, including the Douglas fir, grow here. Patches of quaking aspen can also be seen from the train.

The west slopes of the mountains, on the other hand, have a tropical deciduous forest. This is a low forest of stocky, broad-leafed trees. Generally notable from the train are the amapa, morning glory tree, palo blanco, and a variety of legumes.

Along most of the west coast of Sinaloa, and some of southern Sonora, the semi-arid maritime plain is covered with a thorn forest where it has not been cleared for agriculture. The vegetation is dense, scrubby, often only 20 to 30 feet high, with nearly every bush and tree loaded with thorns. Legumes are dominant, particularly acacias. Leaves are shed during the dry season and the appearance is not very appealing. But winter moisture brings out the spring flowers, and the summer rains cause the foliage to burst forth again in autumn. At such times the thorn forest is attractive and has a charm of its own.

What are some of the important factors which contribute to the rich variety of plant life found along the *F. C. Chihuahua al Pacifico?*

Now and again the earth has a diastrophic movement as a consequence of some pains in the earthly innards. Long, long ago, and even nowadays on occasion, these resulted in the wrinkling of the thin skin-like crust. The tops of the wrinkles became ridges or mountains; the grooves between, valleys. A series of these grouped together, became a mountain range. If the action occurred near the coast, a depression was formed below the sea. Some of the world's best harbors are found in such areas of subsidence. San Francisco is one; Topolobampo is about to become another.

As the wrinkles grew higher, they became cooler and more rain fell if they didn't become too high. If they grew high enough to have peaks and ridges covered with perpetual snow, and were far enough south to have tropical seas washing the low folds, conditions were sufficient to satisfy the requirements of most known plant life. Here, in a few thousand vertical feet, would be found life zones which would require hundreds of miles of latitude to duplicate.

Most of these life zone conditions are found in the country traversed by the *Chihuahua al Pacífico*. The Arctic Zone is not represented however, and the tropical is intrusive but not lush.

A map of plant distribution in Mexico is more complex than a map of physiographic features. Both are generalized and can't show local variations. Even so, many plants are very flexible and can survive, or even thrive, in a wide variety of habitats. These can be found growing high on the slopes, or approaching the sea, as well as flourishing where conditions are optimum. So even a generalized map of plant distribution must be more complicated.

The plant associations and classifications are an aid to understanding, and are broadly true. But, to caution again, it is necessary to remember that there are few sharp lines of demarcation in nature. Rather there are countless areas of intergradation where species intermingle, now with certain types, now with others. The most constant situations seem to be those where life factors are limited and vary but little, such as the *bolsones* where there is low rainfall, hot weather and regular flood. Here, too, there is limited life.

This, fortunately, is not the common condition along the *F. C. Chihuahua al Pacífico*. Along its route are most life zones, as well as a great variety of vegetation to interest the student or traveler. There is a long spring, by reason of the changes of elevation. Plants and trees blossom after the winter fall of moisture. The summer rains result in a flourishing foliage in the fall. Autumn brings, in the higher areas, bright patches of color and sparkling air. Yes, spring and fall supply the best of the year.

ANIMAL LIFE

The dedicated sportsman who boards the train at Ojinaga does not expect much of interest to engage his attention for many miles. He notes the ubiquitous jack rabbit, while dozing and traveling over the plains. A covey of quail scurrying for cover makes him open his eyes. But he becomes fully awake with sparkling eye when he sees a small herd of antelope speeding away from the track.

When he reaches Chihuahua City he learns much more from inquiry. The casual observer is not going to notice many wild mammals where the railroad runs. Some have moved away because of the road, many are reduced in numbers, and a trained eye is frequently required to spot them. A list of animals which has very wide distribution in Mexico, some even country-wide, is: opposum, cottontail, coyote, wolf (northern part), gray fox, ring-tail cat, raccoon, skunk, puma, bobcat, peccary, and white-tailed deer. Some found mainly in plains country of the north: antelope, mule-deer, and badger. Big-horn sheep are also in the north plains, mountains, and deserts, wherever there are crags for protection. The grizzly bear is scarce in the United States, but fairly large numbers of them still live in some mountainous areas 50-75 miles north of the city.

When making personal inquiries, the sportsman was referred to several books and articles. These pointed out that some animals are specialized as to habitat while others live in many different situations. Such are adaptable and thus have a wide range. Another fact learned is that ultimately all animals are dependent on plants. The meat eaters, or predators, prey on animals which live on plants. So, no plants, no animals.

Also, the more people there are, the fewer animals. The population of Mexico has tripled since 1900. This increase has put tremendous pressure on the land. Vegetation has been greatly modified, even radically so. In fact, there are substantial areas in which erosion following upon over-use has created desert-like wastes where, formerly, vegetation flourished. Conservation of land is a major problem in Mexico, and a national effort on a broad front will be necessary to meet it. A simple thing, like gathering firewood for cooking and heating, is a major cause of over-use of land and vegetation. Gas for fuel could alleviate this problem.

Whenever a significant change in vegetation occurs, the effect is to change the habitat, the home, of animals. Most are affected adversely, a few favorably. The number of deer, quail, and rabbits will increase with some opening up of wooded land. But their increase is matched by a reduction of those animals whose habitat has been modified adversely. Hence, wild animal life is not as abundant in Mexico as it used to be.

Nevertheless, outstanding hunting is still to be found in certain areas of Mexico. In the area of the *F. C. Chihuahua al Pacífico*, the best hunting (for mammals) is along the Madera Division, which is a good approach to the northern plains, uplands, and mountains of that region. A note was made of this for a future expedition.

This time the trip was by the direct line to the coast, so the next region to be of intensive interest is the mountain-barranca home of the Tarahumara Indians. The sources of information suggested to the sportsman that he would be best instructed by learning from the Tarahumara, so he arranged to break his rail trip at Creel for the purpose.

Almost any animals are meat for the Tarahumara's pot. But, as do most people, they deny liking to eat crow. The animals and birds mentioned thus far are used by them if found in their country. They are diligent, too, about looking for them, and are good hunters.

Also eaten, when available, are pheasant-like birds called *pui*, cranes, swallows, magpies, and even hummingbirds. Birds taken principally for their feathers are *pito neal*, ivory-billed woodpeckers, and macaws.

The Indians fish extensively wherever water is available. The fish are, naturally, fresh water species. And they do not overlook amphibians and reptiles.

Besides the mammals listed above, the Tarahumaras also take, by various methods, and use for food or other purposes, the following: hares, gophers, coati mundis, black bears, insects, bees for honey, fox squirrels, and rodents. Mice are highly prized.

Among the poets of the East, the Mediterranean area, and Western Europe, the eyes of their beautiful women have been likened to the stars, the eyes of an ox, a faun, or a doe. The Tarahumaras liken theirs to the limpid eyes of a mouse. This should qualify them, too, as pretty close observers of nature.

The present range of wild turkeys is the high country of the pine-oak forest, where mast, a major food item, is available. They have possibly half the range of earlier times before human population pressure pushed them back.

Mexico has some species of quail in almost all of its parts — mountain, coast, plain or desert. So several are found in railroad country.

An interesting bird frequently tamed, is found on the coast, and into the foothills of the west mountain slope. This is the *chachalaca*. It is more common farther south, and is a reminder of the tropical quality of the coastal section of a part of northwest Mexico.

There are many species of dove in Mexico, but by far the most important game birds are mourning and white-winged doves. Both have a wide distribution, but the former are more concentrated in the arid, temperate uplands, while the latter are more numerous along the coast. There are also considerable numbers of other members of the pigeon-dove family.

Ducks and geese are still found in tremendous numbers along the coast, especially around the excellent fishing waters of Topolobampo. A good place to arrange for these sports was found to be the Hotel Santa Anita of Los Mochis. But there are not as many ducks and geese along the coast as formerly, while the numbers of birds found in the highlands of the northern interior are still more reduced.

The coast region animals are: gray squirrels, deer, river otter (extends up river drainages), jaguar, ocelot (range into central Sonora), and jaguarundi.

When the sportsman had reached Los Mochis-Topolobampo, the western terminus of the *F. C. Chihuahua al Pacífico*, and completed his survey, he concluded that this region was best for fishing and bird shooting, although good sport in larger game is to be found here. However, the Madera Section is superior for the latter, and a convenient place for arrangements is Casas Grandes in Northwest Chihuahua.

Railroad store.

The Tarahumaras

Let us go quickly to the southwest part of Chihuahua which on the *F. C. Chihuahua al Pacífico* is known as the Mountain or Sierra Division. This is the mountain-barranca country, and is the heart of the homeland of the Tarahumara Indians. For this reason, it merits an extended visit. Please remember that this region offered the most difficulty for building the railroad. Here the engineering problems were greatest and the costs most prohibitive. Hence, it was the last section completed.

Before the grading and construction began, a right of way was established. Along this way in the fifties, it was a common sight to see individual ties at intervals, lying gleaming in the sun on the hillsides. Soon I saw how this was done.

A Tarahumara Indian with an axe approached a 12-inch log sawed to tie length. Along one side of the log he used his axe to score it to a depth of an inch and a half, at intervals of several inches. This took ten to twelve seconds — one burst of my spring-wound movie camera. An equal amount of time was taken to use his axe like an adze and chip off this side of the log to a flat plane. The process was repeated three more times and a relatively smooth tie with four flat sides was the result. This was indeed a skillful piece of business, and at ten cents a tie, such a man could make excellent wages.

For me, at any rate, he became the symbol of this part of the railroad. He bridges the techniques from the old to the new. When hard labor and hand tools were the requirements, as in the earlier days of construction, he filled these needs with good cheer. When more skilled labor was needed to operate great earth moving machines, he learned to operate them, for he was flexible and smart, as well as hard working. The railroad was running through his country, and he did much to make it his road.

By now one might be curious as to "who is a Tarahumara?"

A simple answer, frequently given by popular writers, is that he is the last of the cave dwellers. The implication, therefore, is that he represents a final link with man's prehistoric past, and for this reason, is an item of curiosity. It would be a mistake to accept such an estimate. Like many simple answers, it is highly misleading.

He has also been called a foot-runner. In fact, this is what he calls himself — Raramuri. *Tarahumara* is regarded as an obvious corruption of this word, and the historical literature refers to him in this way. It would be difficult to find a better single-word name, for footrunning is one thing that is characteristic of all Tarahumaras.

He has also been called the Indian of the barrancas, or canyons, areas which lie in one of the most remote parts of Mexico. This is rough country, and a demanding environment. To live in such an environment has required just about perfect adaptation, since even small errors can be critical; and big ones, fatal.

Consider this quotation from Pennington. "The material culture of the Tarahumara today represents an example of an intelligent and complex use of a rather inhospitable environment, and it is very clear that, although almost four centuries of contact among the Indians, Spaniards, and mestizos have brought about changes, modifications, substitutions, and abandonment of certain aspects of the Tarahumara material culture, the basic pattern of settlement, population, and economy has remained essentially unaltered."

So he is not a rude figure from a primitive past. But he is shy, extremely modest, and not very easy to know. He is in the barranca region partly as the result of pressure, partly as a matter of choice. He is very much an individualist, electing to live his life his own way, and has been willing to pay the price.

Now, the railroad has come. It cuts through the very heart of his country, where, in considerable isolation, he had been able to live in his own way. Radical changes in this mode of life are to be expected. How much longer will one be able to see the Tarahumara in native dress, scurrying for cover while herding sheep and goats on the canyon slopes, or beating a drum while traveling along a trail a respectful distance from you?

My first sight of Tarahumaras was an unforgettable tableau. I approached a street intersection in the center of the city of Chihuahua. A Tarahumara family — father, mother, and small boy — passed the corner and suddenly stopped in their tracks and stared. So I stopped and stared also.

Here in the midst of a busy and sizeable city, filled wth people in modern dress, they were in Tarahumara heartland costume: father and son in diaper-like loin cloths, shirts, poncho-like cotton garments, headbands, and blankets; mother in full red skirt, white shirtwaist, red bandana, and blanket; all wearing sandals made of sections from automobile tires. They were remarkable and picturesque, but more remarkable was the singularity and intensity of their alertness. The impression was that they were on an intellectual "point," as intense as a fine bird dog scenting a quail. Some activity of city life engaged their acute and undivided interest for more than five minutes before they moved on. Never had I seen any traveler show such a degree of concentration.

I was a tourist, and they were tourists, and we met in the streets of Chihuahua. It struck me that they were my superiors as travelers, because they probably saw more and learned more than I. Imagine my astonishment to learn later that they may have come from a distance of well over 100 miles, and had covered the round trip in several days! Certainly they were foot-runners, and may well have been cave dwellers too.

This was in 1957. I was, for the first time, about to visit the central part of the Tarahumara country, the upper Río Urique drainage, and the meeting just described, heightened my anticipation. One or more visits a year since then have added to my knowledge and appreciation of these unique people.

But first, a few glimpses into the background of these people — information drawn from studies made by professional observers. Very little archaeological work has been done, and this mostly in the canyons. The earliest known residents go back about 2000 years, and it is assumed that these were ancestors of the present inhabitants.

From these limited archaeological findings it is necessary to jump to the historical record. The Spaniards arrived in the Chihuahua region in the sixteenth century, and found the Tarahumaras in some choice areas. Missionary activity began early in the seventeenth century. At this time, the Tarahumaras occupied most of the southwest quarter of present state of Chihuahua. The terrain includes many features: basin and range, plains and foothills, upland and canyon country. As these features suggest, some of this was prime country for ranching; so ranchers pushed in, and the Tarahumaras gave way to the west and occupied even lower areas of the barrancas, mostly the drainage of the Río Fuerte and its tributaries. They were also squeezed out of some of their northern country, since it too was good range land. By the beginning of this century, their habitat was mainly that of the mountains and canyons — remote, isolated, and harsh country in which to win a livelihood.

Not all of this migration was done peaceably. There were great rebellions. The missionaries and Spaniards were hard pressed but persistent, and eventually the most intransigent of the Tarahumaras gave way to the west and southwest. It is thought, however, that some stayed on and were absorbed, becoming part of the mestizo or mixed-blood culture of the region.

Those who moved were a tough people and joined their hardy cousins already in the region. Sparse resources were put to more careful use. Amazingly, the general population of the tribe was not seriously diminished, and has remained fairly constant throughout historical times. The total population is estimated to be about 50,000, so the Tarahumaras are the largest tribe of Indians (Mexico) north of Mexico City.

Students have found it convenient to divide them into sierra (mountain) and barranca (canyon) Tarahumaras. These divisions recognize both cultural as well as geographical and environmental differences. Since many spend the summer months on the high plateaus or mountains, and winter in, or part way in, the canyon, there can be many gradations. How much study and how many books it would require to enumerate and describe these is indeed a question.

The observations herein have been obtained in the region most students consider as being purest Tarahumara. It might be called Mexico's Grand Canyon country. Here the scenery is spectacular and the means of winning a living, harsh and scattered.

It is high plateau country with average elevations of 7000 to 8000 feet. Some ridges and peaks are as high as 9000 and even 10,000 feet, and above the line of Douglas fir for this latitude. About 3000 feet of the topmost deposit is volcanic, tuff or lava, as the case may be. A somewhat harder layer of volcanic material overlies this. Folded sedimentary materials are beneath.

The volcanic tuff is fairly soft, hence subject to erosion. Much water erosion has occurred, since precipitation in this upland or sierra region is about 20-25 inches annually. So the country is much cut up into canyons and ridges. The primary canyons have permanent streams of water. Side canyons to these — secondary, tertiary, and so on — are dry most of the year. Nevertheless, small springs, more or less permanent, are found at many places on the slopes of these side canyons. You may find them if you are as smart as a Tarahumara. But it is easier to look for the activity of this knowledgeable fellow. From the rim, with sharp eyes or binoculars, look around to discover corn patches or other signs of human activity on the steep slopes. When you have located such, it is likely that some sources of water, although it may be seasonal, is nearby.

From the steeply sloping field, follow with your eye along a path. It may lead to a cave dwelling.

This is great country for the production of caves because of the harder volcanic layers over softer volcanic tuff. Water and other erosional factors wear away the soft materials and leave the more resistant overhang. In time, a fine cave results. Along comes a Tarahumara family and makes it a home, albeit temporary. Nearby can be found their fields or grazing grounds; steep, but suitable for goats and even sheep.

The popular writer looking for a sensational slant says these caves represent the backward Tarahumara. I say they represent the smart Tarahumara, since I have been there in stormy weather in late February, and would have welcomed a sheltered cave for comfort. So would have my highly educated companions, after having nearly smothered in their pup tents following a five-inch snowfall.

Just to get the record clear, even in this barranca country, a substantial majority of the Indians can be found living in houses. Houses are of wood, stone, or a combination of both, and come in a variety of styles of construction. It is not probable that any Tarahumara lives in a cave for an entire year, let alone a whole lifetime, even though it might be more comfortable. The reason for this is fairly simple. This is harsh country in which to make a living. When the resources of one area are exhausted, it is necessary to move to another. Only a few upland meadow flood areas can be farmed for more than two or three years. Forage for sheep, goats, and cattle is even more quickly exhausted. So a move to another property becomes imperative. Also, laws of inheritance are such that a Tarahumara family commonly has a number of fields and patches, more or less widely spaced, since inheritance follows the female as well as the male line. Usually all children share in an inheritance from father and mother. So property is scattered, and this makes for a life of movement. Thus all available resource is utilized. Anything less could prove critical.

The basic foodstuffs are corn, beans, and squash, supplemented by some animal products — goats, sheep, and cattle, including oxen. In addition, very few things which grow, swim, or fly are neglected. If not utilized by the Indians, they are ingested by the animals and used as fertilizer for the fields and gardens.

As practical botanists, it is difficult to beat the Tarahumaras. One may recall that between the sierras and the canyons there is an altitudinal range of something over 5000 feet. Several life zones are represented here, hence a considerable variation of species of plants, as well as animals.

For comparison, just consider that a student can receive a college degree, and become a professional forester on one taxonomic course, which includes about 150 trees and shrubs, plus another one or two courses which give some familiarity with a dozen or so grasses. Much of this material is forgotten, because not used, although some additional botany is usually learned in the field.

Tarahumaras, on the other hand, use more than 50 plant items as mixes and condiments to add interest and variety to their food. In order to catch fish by stupefaction, they know the use of more than 30 plants.

They collect more than 50 fruits and nuts, about 20 varieties of seeds, over 60 varieties of edible greens and leaves, approximately 20 kinds of roots, and a dozen miscellaneous items such as mushrooms and fungi.

The most important beverage is *tesguino,* most commonly made from maize (grain or stalk), but over 20 additional plants, fruits, or seeds may be used on occasion. About 23 additives or catalysts are used to make the tesguino strong. The use of this drink is dependent upon availability and flavor. The "mixed drink school" may be correct. It is said that the only time a Tarahumara's sense of direction is at fault in this extremely cut up country, is when he has had too much to drink.

Other plant knowledge is utilized for incense, batons, musical instruments — drums, reeds, rattles, rasping sticks, and violins.

For medicinal purposes, they draw from 53 plant families! Many unidentified specimens are also used. Varieties are much more numerous. These are used for pulmonary troubles, urinary disorders, backache, menstruation pains, cough, rheumatism, foot infection, malaria, constipation, festering sores, heart ailments, stomach upsets, wounds, intestinal disorders, intestinal worms, heat prostration, toothache, elimination of fleas, lice, and ticks upon man or beast, kidney disorders, gonorrhea (infrequently afflicted because of aloofness from other peoples), sleeplessness, jaundice, sore throat, earache, conception, diarrhea, bruises, bites, and other maladies. Between the shamans and grandmothers, almost everything is represented but psychiatry. Some of them still have peyote, even though they have to go almost to Texas near Ojinaga, a distance of several hundred miles, to get it.

Very few animals escape their attention. Some are taken for food only, while others supply some other part of their needs. Other animals are destroyed because they prey on domestic animals or damage crops or stores.

Many birds are taken, but the wild turkey is most important. Sometimes it is captured and tended until quite tame.

Cottontails, hares, squirrels (arboreal and terrestrial), gophers, small rodents (mice are regarded as a great delicacy), otters, badgers, skunks, raccoons, ring-tailed cats, coatis, opossums, foxes, peccaries, and deer are the most common animals hunted. But insects are not scorned, nor are amphibians and reptiles.

Methods of hunting include use of hands, various traps, bow and arrow, lances or sharpened sticks, rocks thrown by hand or with sling, running down, and some use of firearms. Deer are commonly run down, and running down rabbits is regarded as much a sport as food gathering.

Fish are an important food item, particularly when there is crop failure, as well as between crops. They are caught by use of hands, bows and arrows, lances, traps, poison, and sometimes by detonating dynamite caps.

It is already quite apparent that a lot of skill, know-how, and general alertness is required to make a living in this country. Also required is a lot of hard work.

One student said that a woman never sits idle, which fits the old rhyme that "woman's work is never done." This is something of an exaggeration, since there is quite an amount of fun in Tarahumara life, however hard it is. But women grind corn, boil beans, look for herbs, weave, take care of the children, and are generally regarded as devoted and loving mothers. As part of the entire family, a woman helps with weeding and harvesting the crops. Herding and milking the animals often falls to her lot. She gives some care to the house and the dancing platforms, and has a good many duties in connection with feasts and ceremonies.

At the beginning of a new day, she and her husband talk over the plans to be followed. Since she may own at least half of the property, this is not surprising. And her advice and approval are required for making a deal or sale. But so is that of the children, even the small ones. To obtain a child's approval often requires a selling job on the part of the parents, so to buy a sheep may require two days. And if a pet is involved, a child may even refuse to give it up.

Some women talk a great deal and constantly nag their husbands. One incessant nagger, who was ugly to boot, caused an inquirer to ask the husband why he didn't get rid of her. He shrugged and replied, "Well, she is a good worker."

This is also the basic criterion for judging the potential worth of a mate on the part of a woman. A man might be wealthy in cattle and land, and a good runner, but a woman's preference is for a man who works well. Could there be more conclusive proof that this is a demanding and harsh environment in which to eke out a living?

Perhaps the men do the harder work, even though the women are said to be as strong. In this upland country, there are but few places, along streams, which are productive for a period of years. Generally, suitable small patches must be found and cleared of trees. The trees are ringed, cut down, and burned. This is hard work for a Tarahumara who is a mighty skillful man with an ax. After the clearing, the ground has to be dug and planted. Often this is so difficult that the neighbors are requested to help.

A great amount of the time-consuming work among the Tarahumaras is done on a cooperative basis. Pay for this, and other favors, such as loans of animals and tools, is mostly in the form of a *tesguinada*, a feast with some form of tesguino, a drink of low alcoholic content but of abundant quantity.

A "good provider" is expected to get some meat for the spit or pot. Domestic animals are seldom killed except as sacrifices, and wild animals are scarce. To capture a squirrel, a hunter may have to cut down several trees of pine or oak. Even then the squirrel may escape.

Deer sometimes are shot with a gun, or bow and arrow. Not uncommonly, they are run down, and this may take help and a day or two of time.

Such achievements receive fulsome recognition. The women are lavish with praise for the successful hunter. He encourages such notice by repeating in detail how difficult it was to find and get the animal.

The metal ax was brought to his country by the Spanish in the seventeenth century. The Tarahumara himself is a master in its use. With it, boards of smooth proportion are cut, so as to make rodent proof storage structures for crops and other valuables. Presently, railroad ties are cut out on a piecework basis. It takes only a matter of a few minutes for a Tarahumara axman to reduce a round log of suitable length into a four-sided railroad tie. This is a marvelously skillful piece of work, and a pleasure to watch.

When not hunting abroad or working in the field at home, a man makes bows and arrows and plays the violin, his favorite amusement. Please note that he plays the violin stretched on his back. It would be a querulous hag who did not know he was playing partly for her, so she picks up the tempo on a metate grinding corn, produces better meal, and everyone gets better tortillas.

So now you think the woman works harder because, "she must never be lazy." Tarahumara men never get heavy, but some of the women do. (Large fat thighs is a standard for womanly beauty, and a good looking woman is called "a beautiful thigh." But to say she has eyes "like a mouse" is even higher praise).

Near neighbors are frequently called upon to give cooperative assistance with time-consuming and difficult tasks such as clearing fields, building houses, plowing, and some types of hunting and harvesting. Pay, as mentioned before, is in tesguino. There are times when this seems as much an excuse for a fiesta as for need of assistance. The day is given over to hard work, the evening and night to eating, feasting, and much drinking of tesguino. For a Tarahumara, one of the most desirable conditions is that of "a beautiful intoxication."

Tesguino is not drunk, however, unless some purpose is to be achieved. But purposes are numerous. Birth, marriage, death, curing of people, land, trees, even inanimate objects, venerating the gods and the dead, raising houses, beginning a hunt, and making rain constitute a partial listing of purposes. In effect, no important act is engaged in unless tesguino is drunk. Nothing is so close to their hearts. It is an integral part of religion, and is used at all feasts and ceremonies.

One of the times the women out-rank the men is in drinking tesguino. A serving for a man is three gourds full, while a woman gets four. One reason for this custom may be that the girls initiate most of the courting. The famous traveler, Carl Lumholtz, said that without tesguino it is quite possible that the Tarahumaras might have died out because of their excessive modesty and shyness under everyday circumstances.

Usually they are very undemonstrative, particularly in public. This is not true of their relationship with their children, however. They delight in playing with them and show affection by kissing them on the lips and stomach. In public, lovers are very circumspect. They may sit close together, and the woman will hold the forefinger of the man's hand in a secretive way. This is before tesguino, of course.

After a liberal amount of tesguino has been consumed, the tone and tempo of the fiesta changes. According to Lumholtz, the crowd soon becomes jolly and silly, out for a good time, and he enjoyed these occasions himself. But, as might be expected, there was occasional fighting and violence.

Although Tarahumaras frequently leave and rejoin the home group without any salutations, they are regarded as very polite people. Their vocabulary includes expressions of "please" and "thank you," and they never join or leave a social group without some gesture or word of politeness.

It is with reluctance that they part with anything by sale or barter. They have so little that they feel very much attached to a possession. It is considered a favor to part with any belongings for money, and a purchase establishes a kind of brotherhood between negotiants, who afterwards call each other "naragua." In times past, reluctance to sell for anything but coins was a response to unscrupulous traders who paid them in cigarette coupons.

This and other "slights" have earned choice, but well-concealed, scorn for the Mexicans. They say hell is overflowing with Mexicans, hence they come out in the barrancas to harass them. Mexicans are also said to be "hairy like a bear," and have a strong smell. To them, norteamericanos smell like coffee (brand not specified), but the aroma is unpleasing.

Lumholtz said that Tarahumaras have a slight odor too, but are not aware of it. But such is life, with its biases and discriminations. Perhaps tourists should visit them disguised in Yardley's Black Label and Chanel No. 5.

So it seems apparent that a number of Tarahumaras live as they do out of choice, and as an expression of their nature. They want to be isolated and live alone. Now and again, here and there, they congregate into a community or village, but may not remain for long. The missionaries have discovered this. Many Indians seem to welcome the isolation of their demanding environment, with its scattered patches of farmable soil. Here they may live relatively alone except for the feasts and fiestas.

Crafts are not numerous, nor skills remarkable, but they do make baskets and pottery, and weave girdles and blankets.

The children are alert and intelligent, and do well when given a chance to learn. Boys, who get some schooling, and learn to read and write, become ambitious. They dream of becoming generals or even presidents.

Tarahumaras are polite, but not especially hospitable. A visitor approaches, but sits down at a distance to be recognized, even though a friend or relative may be the visitor. The Indians have a saying, "only dogs enter a house uninvited." During a visit, the guest may be fed, but is seldom invited to spend the night inside the dwelling. Only extreme emergencies win such invitations.

They delight in games, and the men and children play almost every day of the year. The women do not play as frequently, since they have less free time.

Games are mainly those of skill or chance, although betting may be involved in any of them. Quoits, wrestling, stick throwing, or archery are examples of games of skill. Gambling games include a dice-like game with animal knuckle bones, and the most popular game is called *quinze*, which is played with four sticks of different value. This is the greatest gambling game. Tarahumaras of means have been known to play it for two weeks or a month, until all property has been lost. There are other games, although all are not everywhere common. Betting may be done by spectators as well as participants.

The "national sport" is foot-running. The men's race involves the moving of a wooden ball, a few inches in diameter, over a prescribed course a given number of times, by kicking the ball after the toes have been placed under it. Two teams of two to twenty are involved, and a ball is given each team. The contesting teams may be local, or from different regions. The winning team is the one which gets its ball across the goal line first, after complying with all regulations including traveling the required number of circuits.

The big races are events of great excitement, and may draw up to 200 spectators. There is lots of betting, and much partisan spirit is shown by the spectators. No one is an uncommitted bystander.

The rules and procedures are complicated. Officials lay out and mark the course. Others are stationed as umpires to assure compliance with course and rules. Teams have managers, and these are often shamans, since it is not supposed that the winners win by natural means. The losers were bewitched.

Training consists of abstinence from women and tesguino (about the only thing for which it is not regarded as effective) for several days. Practice mainly involves kicking the ball. At night the runners are confined and guarded by the elder men.

The courses are at least 14 miles in length. Circuit requirements vary. Many races total 60 to 170 miles, and although started at midday, go well into the night, with the courses marked by torches. At the start, a representative of each team kicks the team ball forward to his mates in advance. One of these performs similarly to the others who have run ahead. So there is a steady, although not swift forward progression of the ball. But the distance involved results in runners dropping out, until the winner who crosses the goal line may be the last man on his feet.

Lumholtz claims that the Tarahumaras are the greatest endurance runners in the world. Taken collectively, this may be quite true, since they have a high percentage of men, women, and children who can run great distances. He says they easily run 170 miles without stopping. One man carried a letter 600 miles (less short cuts) in five days, and lived on *pinole* (ground parched corn meal) and water. So they are fully entitled to their name, "foot-runners."

There is a form of racing for the women too. In this, the women toss a ball or hoop with a stick. Their races lack the importance of the men's, but there is nevertheless much excitement and betting on these occasions as well.

Many things are said of these remote and unspoiled Tarahumaras, who live in the fastness of this inhospitable barranca region. Around the perimeter of this region, many influences have come to bear.

In the eastern region, as is mentioned earlier, many Tarahumaras were absorbed centuries ago. The missions have had a notable effect, particularly at Sisoguichic with its orphanage, school, hospital, and instruction program by radio. Mining in the canyons, and other Spanish and Mexican activity, has had a qualifying effect for decades, especially in the lower altitudes.

Then came the railroads, beginning almost a hundred years ago. Initially their influence was bad, according to the Indians. The peyote gardens were destroyed, and the black clouds of smoke from the engines obscured the Tarahumaras from the benign and watchful care of their principal deity, *Tata Dios,* the sun.

But for the past 30 years the railroad has been a great benefit. Ing. Francisco M. Togno in his early career spent much of his time restoring and building the *F. C. Chihuahua al Pacífico.* Much of the labor, using simple tools of pick, shovel, sledge and drill, was supplied by the Tarahumaras in those early days. As the program progressed through the forbidding canyons, increasingly complex machinery was used, until at last came modern earth moving machinery. The Tarahumaras kept pace with these developments and learned to operate these complex machines. Ing. Togno speaks of these Tarahumaras with respect and affection when referring to their contribution in putting through the railroad. These particular Tarahumaras may be so changed in appearance that it takes a sharp and discerning eye to discover them among the other skilled workers who run and maintain the railroad.

So there are many Tarahumaras. Some step right out of the past, others are very much in the present, and there are a great many variations in between. Most of them are quite intelligent; all are very interesting. Particularly so is the lone figure, in loin cloth and typical back country dress, lounging along the way. In his skillfully unobstrusive manner, he is watching you, and he finds you very interesting. Judging from the foregoing, I have obviously found him to be of great interest, and hope to learn even more about him from personal association.

But to do this, it is necessary to stop and linger awhile. Nothing much is learned from a hasty glance, nor a rapid passage through. How long will these fascinating people remain unspoiled, even though there is little smoke from a diesel locomotive to obscure the watchful care of *Tata Dios?* As diesels increase in number, they bring influences more lasting than smoke.

Canyons Compared

In one sense, to attempt a comparison between such wonders as Arizona's Grand Canyon and Mexico's Barranca del Cobre is an act of presumption. The varieties of personal experience cannot be adequately reflected in a few words. Hence, although the observations to follow may seem quite familiar to those who have visited both of these enchanting canyons, to those who haven't, it is hoped that the remarks herein may present a good general description, even within the limitations implied. The condition in, around, over, and about the canyons varies hourly, daily, and seasonally. Even the years have their cycles, as do the decades. In areas such as these, where time is recorded in geologic terms, a thousand years is but a yesterday. Therefore, any visitor would best approach with patience and perceptivity, for the flat light of noon will change, and the evening of a cloudless day can be an unforgettable experience. And tarry awhile for the glory of the night sky. The more dramatic atmosphere of cloud and storm is certain to enthrall the most cynically blasé. So, the ever-changing gorge becomes an awe and wonder, grand and humbling, glorious and sublime.

It is truly not possible to fully record the moods of these canyons on canvas or film. They are evasive to capture. But certain quantities are measureable such as depth, breadth, and extent, although even these can be elusive.

The region of the Grand Canyon of Arizona, and for that matter, the Colorado River drainage system has been subjected to careful survey and mapping. The maps are available. The barrancas of this part of Mexico have not been mapped, and even such survey information useful to engineers is in short supply. Here and there in some areas, the depth and width of the canyon has been calculated. Now surveys will no doubt make possible a closer comparison of the physical features of the canyons. Meanwhile, the present lack of knowledge has encouraged some rather extravagant statements.

It has been claimed that four Grand Canyons of Arizona could be contained within the Barranca del Cobre section of the barrancas. Even if this were extended to include the larger area of the Fuerte River drainage, it would still not be creditable, no matter how casual the observation. Lack of exact knowledge for comparison nothwithstanding, it is probably true that points from a plateau rim will yield a slightly greater depth for the canyon close by the *F. C. Chihuahua al Pacífico,* than for Arizona's Grand Canyon.

Little is known about comparative widths from rim to rim, although it is probable that the average width of the Grand Canyon of the Colorado is greater. But it is not difficult to see that a greater mass of material has been eroded away in the Colorado River drainage because it has a cross section profile of a series of vertical walls successively narrowing into lower terraces or plateaus, while Barranca del Cobre is quite V-shaped.

There is a famous folk legend which describes how Paul Bunyan and Babe, his faithful Blue Ox, gouged out the Grand Canyon on one of their journeys by dragging his peavy behind him. Now, if Paul Bunyan had been offered a choice of contract to refill the Grand Canyon or the Barranca del Cobre, my feeling is that he would have selected the latter as being the easier.

Even the entire drainage system of the Fuerte River is not comparable to that of the Colorado River, neither in terms of area drained nor in length of river and quantity and force of flow.

Both canyons are over a mile in depth for considerable distances. In the vicinity of Pamachic, the Barranca del Cobre (this term is increasingly applied to the canyon of the Urique River, and not just a section of the upper part) has a depth exceeding 6500 feet. Arizona's Grand Canyon is commonly said to have a depth of one mile, the point of reference being the southern rim near Park Headquarters. The fact is usually not considered that ten miles away, on the opposite rim, the rim is a thousand feet higher.

It has been indicated in several ways that the cumulative knowledge about the canyons is much more extensive for the Grand Canyon of Arizona. This particularly applies to the field of geology. Few areas have received such intensive study; none have yielded such a wealth of information. It is probably safe to predict that the Barranca del Cobre will never yield such vast material, even when thoroughly investigated.

Remember, the upper deposits consist of about 3000 feet of volcanic material. Associated peaks and higher ridges are also mainly volcanic. The contribution which volcanic material can add to the geologic story has relative limitations.

On the other hand, the upper layers of deposits in the Arizona Grand Canyon are mainly sedimentary and they tell a long, rich story. Moreover, associated studies made on the nearby Red Mountain plateau, add several thousand feet of additional sedimentary history. So, although the Barranca

85

del Cobre cannot be expected to provide as much geologic information, it will yield on thorough investigation much valuable data.

What about the streams in the canyons? The Urique River, as glimpsed from the lookout point at Divisadero, is not many miles from its source. Except in time of flood, it is an insignificant stream. The Colorado River, on the other hand, resembles a sleeping giant even in its low water phase and this is not surprising because it drains a vast area of thousands of square miles.

Annual precipitation in the local park areas (Mexico has not *yet* given park status to the Divisadero area) is comparable. But the amount which actually falls within the canyon rims is apparently much heavier in Mexico. Consequently, much more vegetation is found on the slopes of the Barranca del Cobre, from top to bottom. The plateau vegetation is similar, when due allowance is made for variation of latitude and distribution of plant types.

Animals can be assumed to be in greater variety and number in the barrancas by reason of more vegetation, although they are constantly hunted by the resident people.

Inhabitation constitutes one of the most notable differences. Many thousands of people visit the Grand Canyon every year, and have done so for many years. Relatively few have visited the Barranca del Cobre, although their numbers are increasing. However few people live, or actually have lived, in the Grand Canyon and these have been highly localized, while the Barranca del Cobre is extensively, if sparsely populated. Allowing for this sparseness, it is inhabited from top to bottom, where areas are habitable. It is the home of the Tarahumara Indians as well as increasing numbers of other people. More will follow the railroad.

Following the railroads is a good way to see these natural wonders, the Grand Canyons of Arizona and Mexico. For the past several years our rail tours have made it possible for people to compare personally the two greatest canyons in the world, during a trip called the Canyon Wonderland Rail Tour. This includes several days of stopovers.

While near Divisadero for a few days, the party members have had a fine opportunity to get acquainted with the local people – men, women and children. Tarahumaras and mestizos. The children have been so appealing that a wonderful rapport has always ensued.

In the fall of 1964 a school had just been started and the teacher brought the children to visit us as part of their education. We fascinated them; they intrigued us. Before we left a collection for the school was made. When we returned in 1965, volunteer local labor had erected a new

Curving bridge near Santa Barbara. Mexico Obras Publicas photo.

school building to the roof line. Another collection was made to finish it. Now the building is finished and the name is "Friendship School." We have already observed that Tarahumara children are intelligent and become ambitious when educated. The boys often dream to become a General or a President. It is a thought worth nurturing that from such a simple beginning as a Friendship School, might come future leaders of Mexico.

How to Visit

Dr. Samuel Johnson in effect said that every man of education and attainment got as much Greek as he could, for the added knowledge of Greek language and literature added so much to his general attainment. A paraphrase of similar import can be made about Mexico's "Grand Canyon" and the *Chihuahua al Pacífico* railroad. Every man should get as much of them as he can; they are such a tremendous and valuable experience.

Beginning in 1963, I have operated over a dozen rail tours on which we "Pullman camped" in the back country, spending five days to reach Topolobampo. These were improved by using, too, an open gondola car the last three tours. These were great trips and very comfortable.

Now, a new and superb way has been scouted to visit this region, literally in greater depth. This will be by private EXCLUSIVE autovia (diesel powered passenger coach) on a non-scheduled basis, so that we stop, view and photograph anytime the scene develops. The autovia movement is fitted into the regular train schedules by the operating crew.

We are quartered in rustic lodges at night and provided with food by them. At some overnight stops there are additional features in the area to visit. So we stay as long as necessary to do so, and reach these points of interest by minibus or truck. In fact, from one of these headquarters stops, we expect to get to the floor of the Barranca del Cobre at Urique, where the canyon is deeper than the Grand Canyon of Arizona.

Ten great days are spent on a series of tours, spring and fall. A few hard knocks are to be expected to do these splendid trips which aren't just tours but adventures. Be among the first to have such experiences and write, Wampler Tours, Box 45, Berkeley, Calif. 94701, U.S.A.

To these adventures has been added a new trip which uses regular scheduled train service. It does not spend as much time on side trips nor go as deep into the Barranca del Cobre, but does go all the way to Los Mochis, then continues by bus to Topolobampo, the western terminus of the F. C. Chihuahua al Pacifico. It, too, is 10 days from and to El Paso. For either tour write **WAMPLER TOURS,** Box 45, Berkeley, CA 94701.

ADVENTURE WORLD TRAVEL. Specializes in tours to Los Mochis via the Chihuahua al Pacifico Railroad. Located in the Holiday Inn downtown El Paso. Buses to Chihuahua leave this office. The 5-day tour is moderate in price, double occupancy. For information and reservations contact Adventure World Travel, 113 W. Missouri Ave., El Paso, Texas 79901; Telephone (915) 532-4946, Telex 749-476.

BALDERAMA HOTELES. The most extensive chain of accommodations along the F. C. Chihuahua al Pacifico: *Hotel Santa Anita,* Los Mochis; *Hotel La Posada,* El Fuerte; *Hotel Mision,* one hour east of Bahuichivo; *Copper Canyon Lodge,* south of Creel. The former two can put you in touch with the splendid hunting and fishing of the maritime plain and the coast at the proper season of the year; the latter two are within reach of the great scenery of

Mexico's "Grand Canyon", and can accommodate groups of more than 20 or small parties traveling separately. Inquire: Hotel Santa Anita, Box 159, Los Mochis, Sinaloa, Mexico; Telephone 2-00-46, Telex 05-354.

CABANAS DIVISADERO. Has a spectacular locations on the very rim of the canyon at the Divisadero overlook. It has 34 rooms (expansion planned), twin-bedded, fire places and panoramic views from the windows. The dining room and lounge also have splendid views of the barranca. The cafeteria has Mexican dishes and is associated with a little shop which has Tarahuamara hand crafts. Operates full American Plan and has walking tours with guides. Inquire: Aldama 407-C (or P.O. Box 661), Chihuahua, Chih., Mexico; Telephone Chihuahua 2-33-62.

CABANAS URIQUE. The only operation which includes an overlook from Gallego Point into the barranca at its deepest above the town of Urique 6250 feet below. The cabins are 25 miles east of the railroad, served by private minibus over graveled road, through splendid mountain scenery. Minibus tours to Gallego Point and into the barranca to Urique, including barbecue lunches. Heated cabins hot and cold running water. Full American Plan. Inquire: Mr. G. E. Beckmann, P.O. Box 622, Chihuahua, Chih., Mexico. Telephone 3-02-53.

CARAVANES DE MEXICO. Trailers, campers, motor homes are secured to flat cars of a chartered train for a four day transit through the mountain-barranca country of the F. C. Chihuahua al Pacifico. Daylight travel at a pokey 20-25 miles per hour; on sidings at night. Your equipment is your home for eating, sleeping, and viewing the magnificent scenery. For more information and schedules: 3801-B North Piedras St., El Paso, Texas 79930.

HOTEL NUEVO. A small, immaculate, comfortable hotel operated by a charming Mexican couple who make every one feel at home and feed you well. Near the station at Creel. The proprietor formerly taught school among the Tarahumaras, hence knows the local Indians well, thus is able to conduct the best tours to areas of interest in the vicinity. Inquire: Creel, Chih., Mexico. Telephone, Creel No. 1.

PARADOR DE LA MONTAGNE. Built several years ago, thus relatively new and quite attractive. Have 35 units with two good beds each. Dining room serves three meals a day. Have station wagons and minibus with drivers who can make guided tours to the region's attractions. Meet all passenger trains. Look for representative at the station, even if you have not made a reservation. Inquire: Allende 116, Chihuahua, Chih., Mexico; Telephone 2-20-62 or Creel, Chih., Mexico; Telephone, Creel, Chih., No. 5. English spoken.

POINT SOUTH CARAVAN TOURS. Features trips of varying lengths through Mexico, Yucatan, Caribbean, and Central America. Your recreation vehicle is your home. Expert and experienced leadership provided. All year. A spectacular is "piggy-back" on flat cars of your recreation vehicles through Mexico's "Grand Canyon". All tours feature extremely competent staff, *including a tour leader and mechanic*. For full details (60-page brochure, FREE). Please Inquire: Mr. & Mrs. Dick Petrick, 5309-JW Garden Grove, Tarzana, CA 91356; Telephone (213) 344-8687.

POSADA BARRANCAS. Buildings of stone masonry built about 1970, thus relatively new. Rooms with two beds and corner fireplaces. Seven hundred yards from canyon rim (Barranca del Cobre). Serve three meals, and provide guided tours. Extensive stays encouraged to make longer trips by horse-back. English spoken. Passenger train stop. Inquire: Calle 23 No. 2505, Col. Altavista, Chihuahua, Chih., Mexico; Telephone Chihuahua 3-18-93 or 2-91-25.

SANBORN ESCORTED TOURS. These popular eight day tours depart Saturdays from El Paso or Presidio, Texas (near Big Bend National Park). Round trip is fully escorted, spending time in Chihuahua, Canyon Area, Los Mochis/Topolobampo. Rail travel during daylight. Tours also available through Copper Canyon to Baja California or Mazatlan. Sanborn's is considered by many as the finest weekly tour. Inquire: 404 West Seventh St., Austin, Texas 78701, or call any travel agency.

TRACKS TO MEXICO. Operates mostly September through April. Eighteen day rail and road caravan tours, of which six days are by rail, "piggyback" with your trailers, campers or motor homes fastened to flat cars. Special train through the Sierra Madre Occidental. Some side trips close to railroad. Then, caravan trips to Mazatlan, Los Mochis, Alamos, San Carlos and Nogales. Inquire: 5001 Alameda, El Paso, Texas 79993; Telephone (915) 779-3002.

TRAVEL AGENCIES. Assist operating various tours and can make individual arrangements. *Rojo & Casavantes*, S.A., Bolivar 1000-C, Chihuahua, Chih., Mexico; Telephone 2-60-30 or 2-88-93.

Viajes Flamingo, Hotel Santa Anita, Hidalgo 419 Pte., Apartado Postal 1034, Los Mochis, Sinaloa, Mexico; Telephone 2-16-13 or 2-19-39.

Now, some of you will prefer to do this kind of thing more on your own. Then get in touch with Sr. Pedro Gonzáles, Traffic Manager, Chihuahua Pacific Railway Co., P.O. Box 46, Chihuahua, Chih., Mexico, Telephone 2-22-84. You will receive prompt information about how to do so.

You may even arrange to take your car by putting it on a freight flat car, but do not expect it to accompany you on your train. The services required do not overlap. Anyway, from considerable experience, you can expect friendly attention and prompt consideration.

For the "car-loose" traveler, below is reproduced the most recent schedules of F. C. *Chihuahua al Pacífico* passenger operations between Ojinaga-Chihuahua-Los Mochis-Topolobampo. ¡Buen Viaje!

Tourists going "piggy-back".

Appendices

ITEMS OF INTEREST

The distance between Ojinaga and Topolobampo is 938 kilometers which is roughly 569 miles, figuring a kilometer as .6 of a mile.

Although, some rough country, making engineering difficult, is found between Chihuahua and La Junta, the great construction problem was the Sierra Division, the barranca country. Eighty-nine tunnels were required. "El Descanso" is the longest at 5,928 feet. Three additional tunnels are about ½ mile in length, and three are over 1000 feet long. Length of tunnels totalled 13,343 meters. Forty-eight bridges and viaducts were constructed and add to a total of 3,677 meters. The longest bridge is over the Río Fuerte with a length of 1,638 feet.

Construction of line through the barranca region was held to a remarkable 2.5% grade. The early plan for this rough region called for a cog railroad.

Wooden ties were used in the mountain-barranca region where timber is plentiful. Cement ties were used in the maritime plain area partly because timber was scarce. However, there was also the factor here of using the newest engineering techniques. The rails were bolted to the concrete ties and rode on plates with rubber cushions. This combined with rail welding makes for a remarkable smooth and quiet ride.

The following statistical tables give a good idea of the growth of freight and passenger traffic shown by the *Chihuahua al Pacífico* since it completed the Sierra Division. Much more growth is expected and facilities are being built or expanded to handle it.

Tour train at Divisadero and country near rim of Barranca del Cobre.

CHIHUAHUA PACIFIC RAILWAY COMPANY
TRAFFIC DEPARTMENT
TIMETABLE OF PULLMAN PASSENGER SERVICE
BETWEEN:

CHIHUAHUA, CHIH. AND LOS MOCHIS, SIN.
EFFECTIVE: MARCH 1ST. 1978.

	SOUTHBOUND		NORTHBOUND
	TRAIN No.8		TRAIN No.7
	LEAVE: TUESDAY		ARRIVE: TUESDAY
	AND FRIDAY.		AND FRIDAY.

KM	No.8	STATION	No.7
	Lv. 9:50 PM.	CHIHUAHUA	Arr. 0:50 AM
322	10:55	SANTA ISABEL	11:47 PM
340	11:11	CHAVARRIA	11:31
350	11:23	SAN ANDRES	11:19
368	11:53	MESA	10:56
382	0:06 AM.	ANAHUAC	10:44
401	0:25	CUAUHTEMOC	10:28
413	0:35	CASA COLORADA	10:16
423	0:47	CIMA	10:04
427	0:50	PEDERNALES	10:00
438	1:00	ROSARIO	9:48
	Arr. 1:15 Lv.	LA JUNTA	Lv. 9:35 Arr.
	Lv. 1:45 Arr.		9:05
462	2:00	MIÑACA	8:49
476	2:20	GONZALEZ	8:30
486	2:30	TERRERO	8:22
498	2:48	SIGOYNA	8:10
503	2:57	PICHACHIC	7:59
514	3:15	ATAROS	7:45
523	3:33	TREVIÑO	7:33
533	3:38	SAN JUANITO	7:24
540	3:57	CUESTA PRIETA	7:15
552	4:13	BOCOYNA	6:56
565	4:34	CREEL	6:36
576	4:51	SANCHEZ	6:15
603	5:32	PITORREAL	5:32
	Arr. 5:57	DIVISADERO BARRANCAS	4:59 Lv.
	Lv. 6:12	DIVISADERO BARRANCAS	4:44 rr
625	6:16	IMG.PCC.M.TCGNO	4:40
	Arr. 6:30 Lv.	SAN RAFAEL	Lv. 4:20 Arr.
	Lv. 6:55	CHIHUAHUICAME	3:50
662	7:16	CUITECO	3:24
		BARUTCHIVO	2:39
684	8:33		
699	8:25	CERROCAHUI	1:43
	Arr. 9:00 AM.	TEMORIS	Arr.1:22 PM.
722	9:24	JULIO ORNELAS	12:40
737	10:00	SANTO NIÑO	12:05 PM.
748	10:18	JESUS CRUZ	11:45 AM.
758	10:39	DESCANSO	11:29
764	10:53	LOS POZOS	11:19
779	11:16	AGUACALIENTE	10:49
791	11:35	LORETO	10:35
808	11:58	LA LAGUNA	10:06
823	12:15	IMG.H.VALDEZ	9:51
839	12:34	EL FUERTE	9:33
	Arr. 1:15 Lv.	SUFRAGIO	Lv. 8:50 Arr.
	1:25		8:40
921	2:10	LOS MOCHIS	Lv. 8:00 AM.

ARRIVE: WEDNESDAY   LEAVE: MONDAY
AND SATURDAY.   AND THURSDAY

(+) TRAIN No.7 HAS A 25 MINUTES ==
STOP AT DIVISADERO BARRANCAS (LOOK
OUT POINT FOR COPPER CANYON).
TRAIN No.8 HAS SAME STOP BUT ONLY
DURING MAY TO SEPTEMBER.

GENERAL INFORMATION
YOUR PERSONAL AUTO MAY BE SHIPPED
BY RAIL TO CHIHUAHUA OR LOS MOCHIS
BY FREIGHT SERVICE, THROUGH
ARRANGEMENTS WITH RAILROAD FREIGHT
SERVICE OFFICE AT CHIHUAHUA CITY,
WITH NOTICE AT LEAST, TWO DAYS BE-
FORE YOUR DEPARTURE.

COST FOR SHIPPING YOUR CAR:
CHIHUAHUA TO LOS MOCHIS: $1,173.00
MEX. CY. WHEN SHIPPING SMALL AUTO-
MOBILES, SUCH AS VOLKSWAGEN, FIAT
(SMALL) RENAULT, DATSUN (SMALL), =
ETC. FREIGHT CHARGES QUOTED WILL
APPLY AT HALF RATE. CARS ARE =
HANDLED BY FREIGHT TRAINS ONLY.
LOADED IN AUTOMOBILE TYPE BOX CARS
TAKING 40 HOURS BETWEEN CHIHUAHUA
AND LOS MOCHIS. FREIGHT TRAINS --
LEAVE CHIHUAHUA AND LOS MOCHIS --
DAILY.
BUS SERVICE ONLY 12 HOURS OF TRAVEL
AND GOOD WEATHER CONSTANT BUS AND TAXI
SERVICE.

FOR MORE INFORMATION AND RESERVATIONS
WRITE, WIRE OR PHONE TO:

MR. F. J. SAENZ COLOMO
TRAFFIC MANAGER
CHIHUAHUA PACIFIC RAILWAY COMPANY
P. O. BOX 46
MENDEZ AND 24TH STREETS
CHIHUAHUA, CHIH., MEXICO.

PHONES: 2-22-84 AND 2-38-67.

LIST OF PRINCIPAL BRIDGES AND TUNNELS
EXISTING ON THE MOUNTAIN REGION OF
THE TRUNK LINE: OJINAGA-TOPOLOBAMPO.

TUNNELS	BRIDGES	KILOMETER POST	LENGHT IN FEET
	PALOMIR	126+420	725.07
1		345+767	400.26
2		346+340	367.45
	VIADUCTO ALDANA	A359+720	367.45
	VIADUCTO ALDANA	A362+800	367.45
	RIO SAN PEDRO	A477+437	298.56
3		555+800	981.96
4		551+875	1,233.86
5		592+238	131.23
6		592+303	104.59
7		599+833	164.04
8		599+201	213.25
9		604+201	213.25
10		604+983	262.67
11		608+767	360.89
12		618+375	418.96
13		632+58	337.33
14		632+927	167.45
15		633+187	369.06
16		638+291	351.05
17		638+556	1,512.47
	LA LAJA	639+213	695.54
18		640+818	1,141.98
19		619+661	364.17
	LA MORA	650+081	644.55
20		650+793	859.58
	SEHUERTAVO	651+469	428.97
21		651+55C	597.17
22		652+345	557.02
23		653+408	733.74

The following four tables from mimeographed
material suppiled by F. C. Chihuahua al Pacífico.

CHIHUAHUA PACIFIC RAILWAY COMPANY
RAIL AND PULLMAN FARES
EFFECTIVE: MARCH 1, 1978.

	FIRST CLASS	FIRST PULLMAN CLASS	ROOMETTE (1)	ROOMETTE (2)	BEDROOM	DRAWING ROOM
CHIHUAHUA TO SUFRAGIO	$ 99.40	121.10	167.20	191.00	238.80	453.70
CHIHUAHUA TO LOS MOCHIS	105.80	129.00	176.10	201.30	251.60	478.00

N O T E S:

1.--ALL TRAINS RUN ON MEXICO'S HORA DEL CENTRO, WHICH IS THE SAME AS CENTRAL STANDARD TIME IN THE UNITED STATES.

2.--TO OCCUPY PULLMAN ACCOMMODATIONS, THE PURCHASE OF FIRST PULLMAN CLASS TICKET IS
   REQUIRED: MINIMUMS: ROOMETTE: 1 (ONE) FIRST PULLMAN CLASS TICKET.
                       BEDROOM: 2 (TWO) FIRST PULLMAN CLASS TICKETS.

3.--EQUIPMENT: SLEEPER: 10 ROOMETTES AND 6 BEDROOMS.
               SLEEPER: 10 ROOMETTES AND 6 BEDROOMS.
               DINING CAR: BETWEEN CHIHUAHUA AND LOS MOCHIS.

4.--RAILROAD TICKETS AND PULLMAN FARES ARE QUOTED IN MEXICAN CURRENCY.

5.--NO RESPONSIBILITY IS ASSUMED FOR ERROR IN THIS TIMETABLE, INCOVENIENCE OR DAMAGE RESULTING FROM DELAYED TRAINS OR FAILURE TO MAKE CONNECITONS, SCHEDULE AND RATES HEREIN ARE SUBJECT TO CHANGE WITHOUT NOTICE.

TUNNELS	BRIDGES	KILOMETER POST	LENGHT IN FEET
54		711+546	402.89
55		713+085	315.62
56		713+478	276.57
	EL TIGRE	713+656	154.56
57		713+683	138.78
58		714+311	385.99
59		714+665	236.71
59-A		714+918	157.48
	EL CAMOTE	715+132	101.38
60		715+336	219.49
61		715+475	414.04
62		716+043	164.04
63		716+320	560.00
	EL CARNERO	716+650	264.94
64		717+054	350.86
64-A		717+357	245.82
64-B		717+601	253.43
	GALINDRO	719+580	305.11
69		721+152	443.90
70		721+353	581.86
71		722+427	160.31
72		722+987	134.51
73		723+275	313.65
74		724+142	165.35
75		725+104	243.93
76		725+553	195.21
77		725+697	165.62
	TINAJA	727+220	431.43
78		727+248	114.17
	SAN PABLO	730+422	779.53
79		739+358	205.62
80		740+289	440.62
81		740+574	134.51
	LA CASCADA	742+366	654.53
	CHINIPAS	744+000	1018.35
82		748+421	307.23
83		749+454	376.20
84		751+338	452.09
	EL FUERTE	774+681	646.81
	SAN JOSE	779+881	143.70
	SAN PEDRO	811+894	84.45
	LA ARDILLA	814+875	79.72
	HORMILLOS	819+404	88.78
		823+478	

TUNNELS	BRIDGES	KILOMETER POST	LENGHT IN FEET
24		554+507	587.27
25		554+770	255.91
	NAVOCHIC	655+328	392.22
26		655+467	566.29
27		655+921	566.93
28		656+522	508.53
	BOCOHUINA	656+781	388.78
	MACHAGACHIC	660+232	468.50
	CUITECO UNO	662+560	209.65
29		662+587	242.78
30		662+970	403.54
31		663+559	246.06
32		665+874	219.82
	BAHUICHIVO	669+123	221.78
33		682+345	278.87
	LAS ESTRELLAS	685+097	78.74
	SMITIAGO	686+746	415.26
	RIO PLATA	687+981	272.97
34		684+982	257.38
35		691+050	268.04
36		692+044	636.48
37		692+336	236.88
38		693+602	1102.36
	VIADUCTO UNO.	694+053	128.94
	GEROCAHUI	694+128	172.90
39		694+672	459.32
40		695+527	1548.23
	SEPTENTRION	697+284	318.08
41		698+739	256.10
42		700+140	2542.65
43		701+163	383.86
	LA PAPA	701+390	255.91
44		701+603	479.00
45		701+765	662.30
46		702+063	2680.45
	EL OSO	703+027	114.83
47		703+021	962.36
48		703+426	308.08
	TEMORIS	707+876	2963.68
	SANTA BARBARA	707+876	214.24
49		709+044	413.52
50		709+962	1143.37
51		710+195	1023.85
52		711+050	657.15
53		711+789	348.26
	MINA PLATA		

CHIHUAHUA PACIFIC RAILWAY COMPANY
TRAFFIC DEPARTMENT

TIMETABLE ON THE FIAT DIESEL RAIL CARS
IN PASSENGER SERVICE BETWEEN:

CHIHUAHUA, CHIH. AND LOS MOCHIS, SIN.
EFFECTIVE: MARCH 1ST. 1978.

SOUTHBOUND		NORTHBOUND
TRAIN No.10		TRAIN No.9
Leave: Tuesday		Arrive: Wednesday
and Friday		and Saturday
Lv. 8:00 AM.	CHIHUAHUA	Arr. 8:40 PM
8:52	SANTA ISABEL	7:47
9:18	SAN ANDRES	7:21
9:52	ANAHUAC	6:48
10:08	CUAUHTEMOC	6:34
10:31	PEDERNALES	6:10
Arr.10:53 AM.	LA JUNTA	Lv. 5:47 PM
Lv. 10:58 AM.	LA JUNTA	Arr. 5:43 PM
11:31	TERERO	5:09
12:04 PM.	ATAROS	4:36
12:16	TREVINO	4:25
12:26	SAN JUANITO	4:16
12:48	BOCOYNA	3:52
1:05	CREEL	3:35
1:51	PITORREAL	2:28
Arr. 2:16	DIVISADERO BARRANCAS	2:21
Lv. 2:31	DIVISADERO BARRANCAS	2:06
	ING.FCO.M.TOGNO	
Arr. 2:48	SAN RAFAEL	Lv. 2:21
Lv. 2:54	SAN RAFAEL	Arr. 1:35
3:28	CUITECO	12:58
3:39	BAHUICHIVO	12:47
4:00	PARAJES	12:24
4:15	CEROCAHUI	12:08 PM
4:32	TEMORIS	11:53 AM
4:51	JULIO ORNELAS	11:30
5:11	SANTO NIÑO	11:08
5:26	JESUS CRUZ	10:52
5:39	DESCANSO	10:39
5:47	LOS POZOS	10:30
6:03	AGUACALIENTE	10:12
6:17	LORETO	9:55
6:47	ING.H.VALLEZ	9:28
7:02	EL FUERTE	9:18
Arr. 7:40 PM.	SUFRAGIO	Lv. 8:36 AM
Arr. 8:20 PM.	LOS MOCHIS	Lv. 8:00 A"

TUESDAY AND	WEDNESDAY AND
FRIDAY.	SATURDAY.

CHILDREN: OVER 5 YEARS AND UNDER 12
YEARS PAY HALF FARE.

FOR INFORMATION OR RESERVATIONS:
WRITE, WIRE OR PHONE TO:

MR. F. J. SAENZ COLOMO
TRAFFIC MANAGER
CHIHUAHUA PACIFIC RAILWAY COMPANY
P. O. BOX 46,
MENDEZ AND 24TH STREETS
CHIHUAHUA, CHIH., MEXICO.

PHONES: 2-22-84 AND 2-38-67.

BAGGAGE: NO CHECKED BAGGAGE HANDLED
ON THESE TRAINS.

TIME: CORRESPONDS TO MEXICO'S HORA
DEL CENTRO.

CLASSES: RECLINING SEAT COACH AND
CHAIR COACH.

NOTES: NO RESPONSIBILITY IS ASSUMED
FOR ERRORS IN THE SCHEDULES
INCONVENIENCE OR DAMAGE ---
RESULTING FROM DELAYED TRAINS
OR FAILURE TO MAKE CONNECTION
SCHEDULES AND RATES HEREIN
ARE SUBJECT TO CHANGES - - -
WITHOUT NOTICE.

BUFFET SERVICE: SANDWICHES, SNACKS,
BEVERAGE AVIALABLE AT
YOUR SEATS.

LIST OF PRINCIPAL BRIDGES EXIST ING ON THE CHINAGA-TOPOLOBAMPO LINE:

NUMBER		KILOMETER POST	LENGHT IN FEET
1	FALOMIR	126+420	728
2	VIADUCTO ALDANA	359+720	330
3	VIADUCTO ALDANA	362+800	503
4	RIO SAN PEDRO	477+437	295
5	LA LAJA	639+213	696
6	LA MORA	650+081	458
7	SENUERAVO	651+469	432
8	NAYOCHIC	655+375	391
9	ROCOHUAINA	656+781	387
10	MACHAGACHIC	660+232	317
11	CHITECO UNO	662+560	210
12	BAHUICHIVO	669+123	222
13	LAS ESTRELLAS	683+097	103
14	SANTIAGO	686+746	169
15	RIO PLATA	687+981	272
16	VIADUCTO UNO	694+053	135
17	CEROCAHUI	694+128	173
18	SEPTENTRION	697+284	315
19	LA PAPA	701+390	134
20	EL OSO	703+071	131
21	TEMORIS	707+676	265
22	SANTA BARBARA	707+876	714
23	MINA-PLATA	710+789	350
24	EL TIGRE	713+656	148
25	EL CAMOTE	715+132	101
26	EL CARNERO	716+653	270
27	GALINDRO	719+580	338
28	TINAJA	727+220	60
29	SAN PABLO	730+442	180
30	LA CASCADA	744+009	662
31	CHINIPAS	748+421	955
32	EL FUERTE	779+881	1638
33	LA LAGUNA	806+586	105
34	SAN JOSE	811+894	144
35	SAN PEDRO	814+875	284
36	LAS ARDILLAS	819+404	80
37	HORNILLOS	823+478	190

CHIHUAHUA PACIFIC RAILWAY COMPANY
TRAFFIC DEPARTMENT

FIAT DIESEL RAIL CAR SERVICE

CHIHUAHUA TO LOS MOCHIS TRAIN No.10	LOS MOCHIS TO CHIHUAHUA TRAIN No. 9
LEAVE: TUESDAY 8:00 AM.	LEAVE: WEDNESDAY 8:00 AM.
AND FRIDAY 8:00 AM.	AND SATURDAY 8:00 AM.
ARRIVE: TUESDAY 8:20 PM.	ARRIVE: WEDNESDAY 8:40 PM.
AND FRIDAY 8:20 PM.	AND SATURDAY 8:40 PM.

TIME CORRESPONDS TO MEXICO'S HORA DEL CENTRO

F A R E S

EFFECTIVE: MARCH 1, 1978

CHIHUAHUA TO LOS MOCHIS

RECLINING SEAT COACH	CHAIR COACH
$177.45	$147.00

LIST OF TUNNELS EXISTING ON THE OJINAGA – TOPOLOBAMPO LINE

NUMBER	KILOMETER POST	LENGHT IN FEET
1	345+767	406.26
2	346+340	387.45
3	355+800	981.86
4	561+875	4,113.86
5	590+305	111.23
6	592+338	104.99
7	592+633	164.04
8	599+833	213.25
9	600+201	227.47
10	604+963	360.89
11	600+767	418.96
12	618+575	377.30
13	632+961	180.45
14	632+927	369.06
15	633+187	351.05
16	638+566	1,512.47
17	640+818	1,141.08
18	649+661	364.17
19	651+793	859.58
20	651+850	597.58
21	652+308	331.36
22	653+408	703.74
23	654+507	587.27
24	654+467	25.91
25	655+467	669.29
26	655+921	566.93
27	656+253	508.53
28	662+587	242.78
29	662+970	103.54
30	663+559	244.06
31	663+874	219.82
32	682+345	278.87
33	682+982	257.38
34	691+050	268.04
35	692+014	636.48
36	692+336	236.88
37	692+620	1,102.36
38	694+620	1,548.23
39	695+827	
40	698+739	256.10
41	700+140	2,542.65
42	701+163	383.86
43		

LIST OF TUNNELS EXISTING ON THE OJINAGA – TOPOLOBAMPO LINE

NUMBER	KILOMETER POST	LENGHT IN FEET
44	701+603	479.00
45	701+765	662.30
46	702+063	114.83
47	703+027	623.36
48	703+227	3,074.15
49	704+758	413.52
50	709+644	114.37
51	709+962	1,023.85
52	710+395	165.15
53	711+050	402.89
54	711+546	316.62
55	713+085	277.57
56	713+478	138.78
57	713+683	38.99
58	714+311	236.71
59	714+665	219.48
59A	714+918	259.49
60	715+136	414.04
61	715+175	414.01
62	716+043	560.00
63	716+320	879.59
64	717+056	63.76
65	717+364	345.80
66	718+029	570.86
67	718+345	305.11
68	718+565	41.90
69	721+152	412.36
70	721+353	160.30
71	721+987	134.51
72	722+027	165.32
73	723+275	311.65
74	724+142	243.09
75	725+104	199.21
76	725+553	431.43
77	725+697	199.21
78	727+218	77.55
79	739+388	205.05
80	740+046	446.62
81	740+446	361.25
82	745+364	318.24
83	753+938	452.92
84		
85		
86	754+630	5,966.54

CHIHUAHUA PACIFIC RAILWAY COMPANY
TRAFFIC DEPARTMENT
January 1, 1960 to December 31, 1977

FREIGHT SERVICE (1962 — 100%)

	Revenue	%		Ton / Km.	%
1960	$ 33,487,807	80.9	1960	254,068,584	77.8
1962	41,402,237	100.0	1962	326,506,772	100.0
1970	94,095,475	227.3	1970	806,345,098	247.0
1972	94,460,563	228.2	1972	802,268,505	245.7
1974	106,327,647	256.8	1974	883,463,862	270.6
1976	167,228,335	403.9	1976	965,667,242	295.8
1977	240,339,738	580.5	1977	1,127,832,456	345.4

	Tons Hauled	%		Avg. Rev. Tons / Kms.	%
1960	1,165,313	99.0	1960	0.1318	103.9
1962	1,176,770	100.0	1962	0.1268	100.0
1970	2,066,589	175.6	1970	0.1167	92.0
1972	2,056,292	174.7	1972	0.1177	92.8
1974	2,252,786	191.4	1974	0.1204	95.0
1976	2,712,347	230.5	1976	0.1732	136.6
1977	2,923,631	248.4	1977	0.2131	168.1

PASSENGER SERVICE (1962 — 100%)

	Revenue	%		Psngr. / Kms.	%
1960	$ 2,263,845	44.7	1960	34,700,589	61.7
1962	5,063,230	100.0	1962	56,283,543	100.0
1970	13,168,953	260.1	1970	124,461,289	221.1
1972	16,662,841	328.3	1972	140,732,475	250.0
1974	18,569,679	366.8	1974	143,884,520	255.6
1976	21,668,486	427.9	1976	128,168,830	222.7
1977	23,550,504	465.1	1977	143,888,160	255.6

	Passengers Handled	%		Avg. Rev. Psngr. / Kms.	%
1960	304,261	88.8	1960	0.0652	72.4
1962	342,819	100.0	1962	0.0900	100.0
1970	539,708	157.4	1970	0.1060	117.8
1972	605,326	176.6	1972	0.1180	131.1
1974	548,804	160.1	1974	0.1290	143.3
1976	487,173	142.1	1976	0.1691	187.9
1977	550,057	160.5	1977	0.1637	187.8

EXPRESS SERVICE (1962 — 100%)

	Revenue	%		Kg. Hauled	%
1960	$1,786,453	92.9	1960	15,558,545	94.2
1962	1,922,696	100.0	1962	16,515,082	100.0
1970	2,919,203	151.8	1970	21,355,000	129.2
1972	3,005,399	156.3	1972	20,293,502	122.9
1974	3,502,203	182.2	1974	20,691,132	125.3
1976	5,282,822	274.8	1976	17,771,744	107.6
1977	6,543,785	340.3	1977	15,863,451	96.1

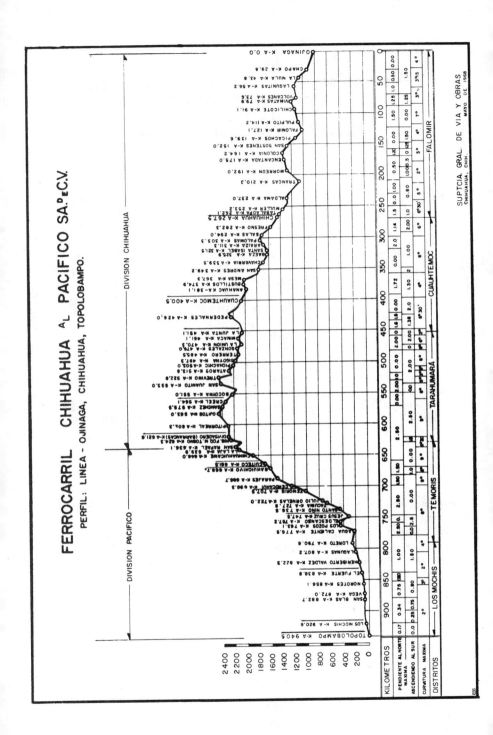

FERROCARRIL CHIHUAHUA AL PACIFICO SA. DE C.V.

PERFIL: LINEA - OJINAGA, CHIHUAHUA, TOPOLOBAMPO.

SUPTCIA. GRAL. DE VIA Y OBRAS
MAYO DE 1968
CHIHUAHUA, CHIH.

97

COMPAÑIA DE FERROCARRILES CHIHUAHUA AL PACIFICO
TREN DE VISTA AMPLIAS
HORARIO
SE INICIA EL PRIMERO DE ENERO DE 1976

LÉASE DE ARRIBA ABAJO

SALIDA: LUNES, JUEVES Y SABADO		LLEGADA: MARTES, VIERNES Y DOMINGO
8:20 AM	CHIHUAHUA	10:05 PM
10:35 AM	CUAUHTEMOC	7:50 PM
1:09 PM	LAJUNTA	7:02 PM
1:53 PM	SAN JUANITO	5:15 PM
3:31 PM	DIVISADERO BARRANCAS	4:28 PM
3:37 PM	SAN RAFAEL	2:32 PM
4:54 PM	BAHUICHIVO	1:31 PM
8:47 PM	EL FUERTE	9:39 AM
9:27 PM	SUFRAGIO	8:59 AM
10:05 PM	LOS MOCHIS	8:20 AM
LLEGA: LUNES, JUEVES Y SABADO		SALE: MARTES, VIERNES Y DOMINGO

LÉASE DE ABAJO ARRIBA

PASAJE

CHIHUAHUA A LOS MOCHIS	$14.20	(dólares)
CHIHUAHUA A DIVISADERO BARRANCAS	7.69	"
CHIHUAHUA A CREEL	6.39	"
LOS MOCHIS A DIVISADERO BARRANCAS	6.50	"
LOS MOCHIS A CREEL	7.69	"

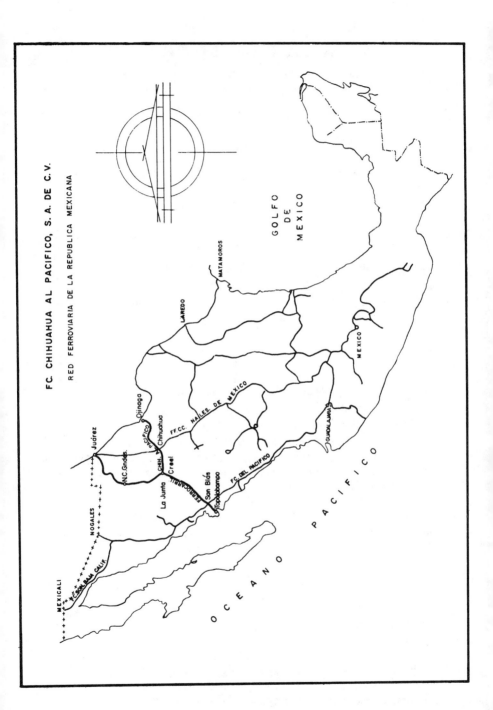

FC. CHIHUAHUA AL PACIFICO, S. A. DE C. V.

RED FERROVIARIA DE LA REPUBLICA MEXICANA

A LIST OF BOOKS

The books listed here, through their references and bibliographies, will take the general reader on long journeys of library exploration.

Almada, Francisco R. *El Ferrocarril de Chihuahua al Pacífico*, Mexico. Editorial Libros de Mexico, 1971.

———. *Resumen de Historia del Estado de Chihuahua*, Mexico, Libros Mexicanos, 1955.

Bennett, Wendell C. and Zingg, Robert M. *The Tarahumara, An Indian Tribe of Northern Mexico*. Chicago, 1935. New printing.

Burgess, Don. *¿Podrias Vivir Como Un Taramumara?*, Mexico, Bob Schalkwijk, 1975.

Dunne, Peter Masten. *Pioneer Black Robes on the West Coast*, Berkeley, 1940.

———. *Pioneer Jesuits in Northern Mexico*, Berkeley, 1944.

———. *Early Jesuit Missions in Tarahumara*, Berkeley, 1948.

Federal Writer's Project. *Texas*, New York, 1940.

Fontana, Bernard L., Edmund J. B. Faubert and Barney T. Burns. *The Other Southwest*, (Indian Arts and Crafts of Northwestern Mexico), Phoenix, The Heard Museum, 1977.

Harris, Harvey A. and Marx, Charles J. *Alamos*, Portland, about 1950.

Hastings, James Rodney — *Climatological Data for Sonora and Northern Sinaloa*, Technical reports of the Meteorology and Climatology of Arid Regions, No. 15, October 1, U. of Arizona, Tucson.

Higgins, III, J. Wallace. *The Railway and Locomotive Historical Society, Bulletin No. 95*, Boston, 1956.

Hollon, W. Eugene. *The Southwest, Old and New*, New York, 1961.

Hovey, E. O. "A Geological Reconnaissance in the Western Sierra Madre of the State of Chihuahua, Mexico", *American Museum of Natural History Bulletin*, XXIII (1907), 401-42.

Jackson, Donald Dale and Peter Wood. *The Sierra Madre*. New York, Time-Life Books, 1975.

Jenkinson, Michael. *Land of Clear Light*. (Wid Regions of the American Southwest and Northwestern Mexico), Dutton, 1977.

———. *Wild Rivers of North America*, Dutton, 1974.

Kerr, John Leeds. *Destination Topolobampo*. (The Kansas City, Mexico and Orient Railway), San Marino, Golden West Books, 1968.

King, R. E. "Geological Reconnaissance in Northern Sierra Madre Occidental of Mexico", *Bulletin of the Geological Society of America*, V (1939) 1625-1722.

Leopold, A. Starker. *Wildlife in Mexico*, Berkeley, 1959.

Lister, Robert H. *et al.* *Archaeological Excavations in the Northern Sierra Madre Occidental, Chihuahua and Sonora, Mexico* (University of Colorado studies, Series in Anthropology, No. 7), Boulder, 1958.

Leviness, W. Thetford. Unearthing History at Casas Grandes, *Americas*, XII: 7:8-13.

Lumholtz, Carl. *Unknown Mexico*, 2 vols., New York, 1902. New printing.

Mares Trías, Albino. *Jena Ra'icha Ralámuli Alué 'Ya Muchígame Chiquime Níliga — Aquí Relata la Gente de Antes lo Que Pasaba En Su Tiempo*, (Taramumara folktales in Tarahumara and Spanish). Mexico, Instituto de Lingüístico de Verano, 1975.

Marshall, James. *Santa Fe*, New York, 1945.

McDowell, Jack (editor). *Mexico*, Lane Magazine and Book Company, Menlo Park, 1973.

Norman, James. *Terry's Guide to Mexico*, New York, 1965.

Peattie, Roderick. *Inverted Mountains*, New York, 1948.

Pennington, Campbell W. *The Tarahumara of Mexico*, Salt Lake City, 1963.

——. *The Tepehuan of Chihuahua, Their Material Culture*, University of Utah Press, Salt Lake City, 1969.

Poors, Manual of Railroads, 1906.

Reeds, S. G. *A History of the Texas Railroads*.

Robertson, Thomas A. *Southwest Utopia*, Los Angeles, 1964.

Sauer, Carl. "The Road to Cibola" *Ibero-Americana, No. 3*, Berkeley, 1932.

Schmidt, Jr., Robert H. *A Geographical Survey of Chihuahua*, Texas Western Press, El Paso, 1973.

Secretaria de Obras Publicas. *Breve Historia del Ferrocarril Chihuahua-Pacifico*, Mexico, 1961.

——. *Memoria de la Construccion del Ferrocarril Chihuahua al Pacifico*, Mexico, 1963.

Spicer, Edward H. *Cycles of Conquest*, Tucson, 1962.

Stilwell, Arthur. *Cannibals of Finance*, Chicago, 1912.

——. *I Had A Hunch*, a Saturday Evening Post, 12-3-27 to 2-4-28.

Sunset, Discovery Book. *Mexico*, Menlo Park, 1963.

Toors, Frances. *New Guide to Mexico*, New York, 1965.

Wallen, C. C. "Some Characteristics of Precipitation in Mexico", *Geografiska Annaler, XXXVII* (1955), 51-85.

Waters, L. L. *Steel Trails to Santa Fe*, Lawrence, University of Kansas Press, 1950.

Weed, W. H. "Notes on Certain Mines in the States of Chihuahua, Sinaloa and Sonora, Mexico", *Transactions of the American Institute of Mining and Engineers*, LXII (1902), 382-407.

West, Robert C. *The Mining Community in Northern New Spain: The Parral Mining District* (Ibero-Americana, No. 30), Berkeley, 1949.

Zingg, Robert M. *Report on the Archaeology of Southern Chihuahua* (Contributions of the University of Denver, III, Center of Latin American Studies I), Denver, 1940.

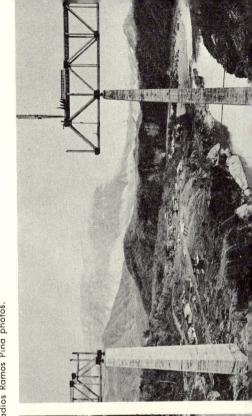

Construction scenes. Eladios Ramos Piña photos.

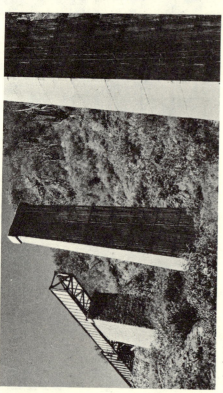

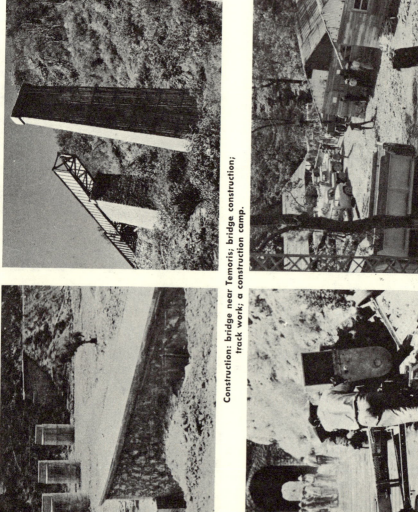

Construction: bridge near Temoris; bridge construction; track work; a construction camp.

(Both pages: Eladios Ramos Piña photos)

Construction: approaching a tunnel; "cat" at work;
laying tracks; track near completion.

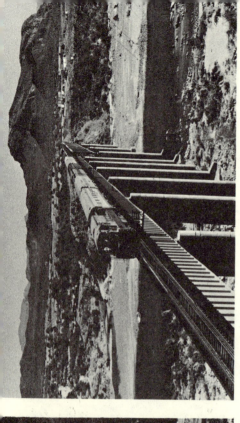

**Bridges: near Temoris; Fuerte River;
Chinipas rail and construction bridges; in Cuiteco.**

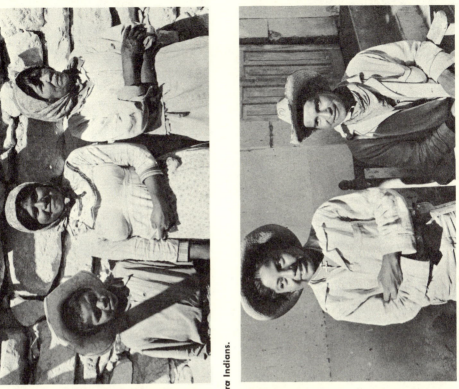

Tarahumara Indians.

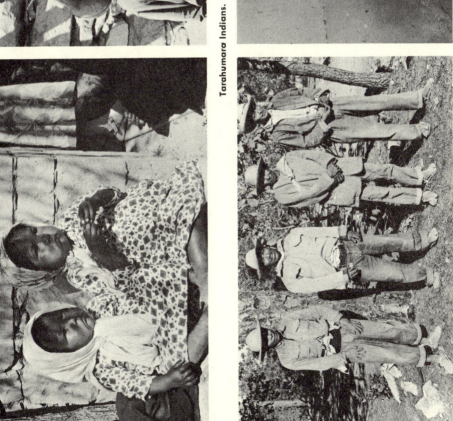

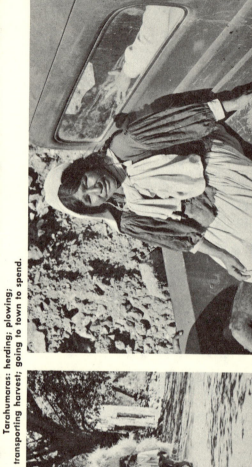

Tarahumaras: herding; plowing;
transporting harvest; going to town to spend.

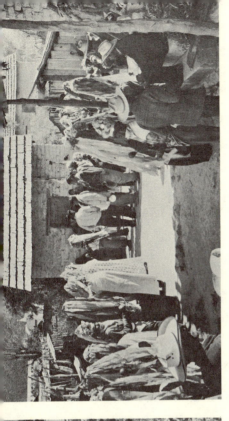
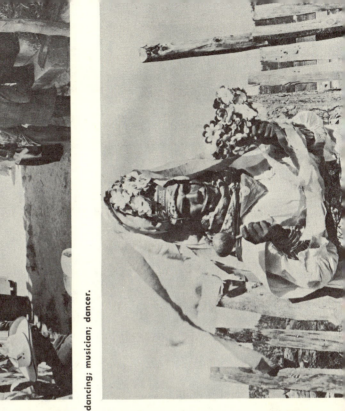

Tarahumaras: gathering; dancing; musician; dancer.

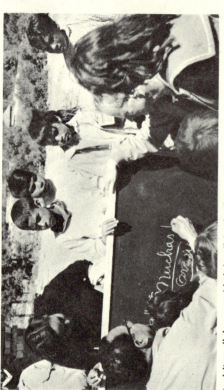

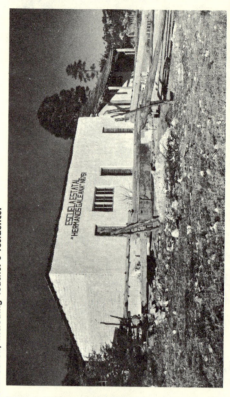

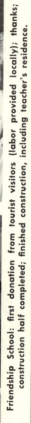

Friendship School: first donation from tourist visitors (labor provided locally); thanks; construction half completed; finished construction, including teacher's residence.

Pottery making: forming; piling; firing; selling.

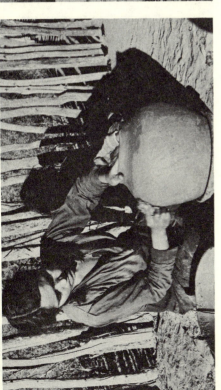

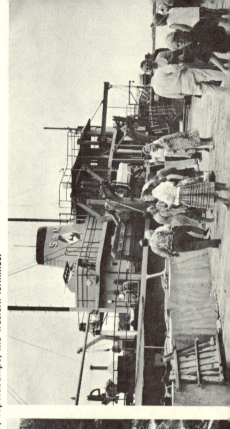

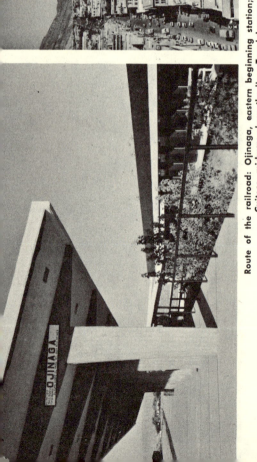

Route of the railroad: Ojinaga, eastern beginning station; Chihuahua, headquarters offices; Cuiteco, midway along the line; Topolobampo, the western terminus.

Towns: Alamos; Creel, old church;
Pancho Villa statue, Chihuahua; growing Chihuahua.

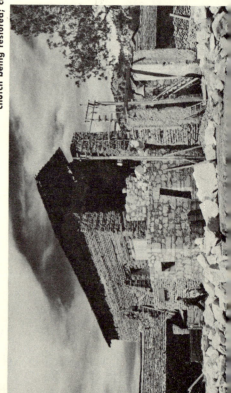

Cuiteco: town of peace, tranquility and apple brandy; homes near church; church being restored; church nearing restoration.

The Fiesta of Christ the King: Entering church; leaving the church for monument.

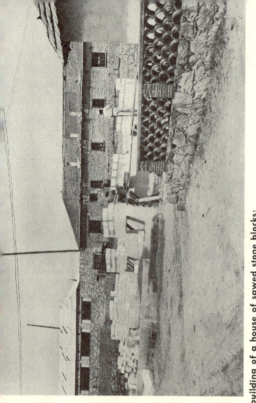

Sisoguichi: a mill for cutting soft rock; the building of a house of sawed stone blocks; boys' dormitory; about Tarahumara portraits.

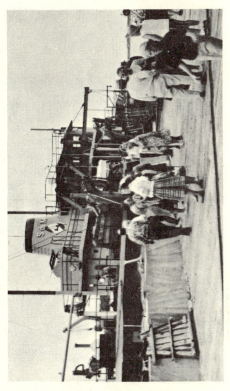

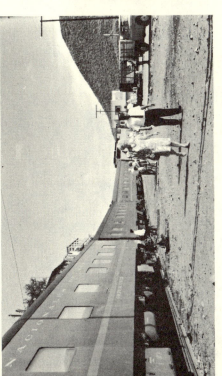

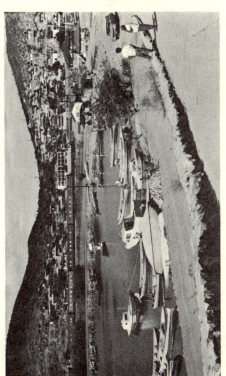

Topolobampo: leaving train; Bay of Bahuia; Inner harbor; at pier.

Late spring snow: Enjoying fire; at canyon rim.

Inside the barranca, part way; at Rio Urique.